CHAPTER 11

Explore 2-Digit Addition

What addition stories can you tell about this picture?

SCHOOL HOME CONNECTION

Dear Family,
Today we started Chapter 11. We will begin to add 2-digit numbers. Here is the math vocabulary and an activity for us to do together at home.

Love,

____

My Math Word

regroup

Vocabulary

When you add two numbers and the total of the two groups of ones is 10 or more, you need to **regroup**. When you regroup, you change a number from one form to another that is equal.

	tens	ones
	1	
	1	6
+		7
	2	3

Add the ones.

$6 + 7 = 13$

Regroup the 13 ones to make 1 ten and 3 ones.

Add the tens.

Visit *The Learning Site* for additional ideas and activities. www.harcourtschool.com

ACTIVITY

Give your child some dimes to stand for tens and some pennies to stand for ones. Choose a number between 11 and 60. Ask your child to show you different ways to make this number with the coins. Repeat with other numbers.

Books to Share

To read about 2-digit numbers with your child, look for these books in your local library.

A Fair Bear Share, by Stuart J. Murphy, HarperCollins, 1997.

The Great Kapok Tree, by Lynne Cherry, Harcourt, 2000.

Name ____________________

Add Tens

What is 30 + 20?

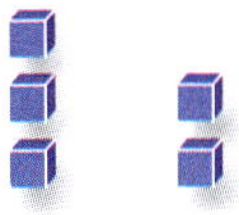

3 + 2 = 5

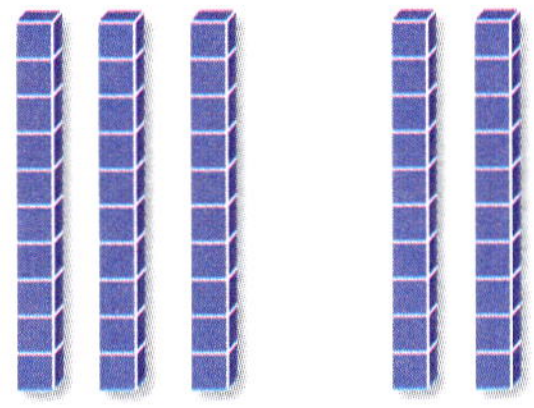

3 tens + 2 tens = 5 tens

30 + 20 = 50

Add.

1

6 + 1 = ______

6 tens + 1 ten = ______ tens

60 + 10 = ______

2

2 + 2 = ______

2 tens + 2 tens = ______ tens

20 + 20 = ______

3

3 + 6 = ______

3 tens + 6 tens = ______ tens

30 + 60 = ______

4

4 + 5 = ______

4 tens + 5 tens = ______ tens

40 + 50 = ______

5

8 + 0 = ______

8 tens + 0 tens = ______ tens

80 + 0 = ______

6

2 + 5 = ______

2 tens + 5 tens = ______ tens

20 + 50 = ______

Talk About It ▪ Reasoning

How does adding 5 tens + 2 tens help you know that 50 + 20 = 70?

Practice

Add.

1. $\begin{array}{r} 2 \\ +3 \\ \hline 5 \end{array}$ $\begin{array}{r} 2 \text{ tens} \\ +3 \text{ tens} \\ \hline 5 \text{ tens} \end{array}$ $\begin{array}{r} 20 \\ +30 \\ \hline 50 \end{array}$

2. $\begin{array}{r} 4 \\ +4 \\ \hline \end{array}$ $\begin{array}{r} 4 \text{ tens} \\ +4 \text{ tens} \\ \hline \text{tens} \end{array}$ $\begin{array}{r} 40 \\ +40 \\ \hline \end{array}$

3. $\begin{array}{r} 1 \\ +8 \\ \hline \end{array}$ $\begin{array}{r} 1 \text{ ten} \\ +8 \text{ tens} \\ \hline \text{tens} \end{array}$ $\begin{array}{r} 10 \\ +80 \\ \hline \end{array}$

4. $\begin{array}{r} 3 \\ +4 \\ \hline \end{array}$ $\begin{array}{r} 3 \text{ tens} \\ +4 \text{ tens} \\ \hline \text{tens} \end{array}$ $\begin{array}{r} 30 \\ +40 \\ \hline \end{array}$

5. $\begin{array}{r} 2 \\ +6 \\ \hline \end{array}$ $\begin{array}{r} 2 \text{ tens} \\ +6 \text{ tens} \\ \hline \text{tens} \end{array}$ $\begin{array}{r} 20 \\ +60 \\ \hline \end{array}$

6. $\begin{array}{r} 3 \\ +3 \\ \hline \end{array}$ $\begin{array}{r} 3 \text{ tens} \\ +3 \text{ tens} \\ \hline \text{tens} \end{array}$ $\begin{array}{r} 30 \\ +30 \\ \hline \end{array}$

7. $\begin{array}{r} 0 \\ +5 \\ \hline \end{array}$ $\begin{array}{r} 0 \text{ tens} \\ +5 \text{ tens} \\ \hline \text{tens} \end{array}$ $\begin{array}{r} 0 \\ +50 \\ \hline \end{array}$

8. $\begin{array}{r} 7 \\ +2 \\ \hline \end{array}$ $\begin{array}{r} 7 \text{ tens} \\ +2 \text{ tens} \\ \hline \text{tens} \end{array}$ $\begin{array}{r} 70 \\ +20 \\ \hline \end{array}$

Algebra

Add.

9. 50 + 30 = 80,
   so 30 + 50 = ______

10. 30 + 40 = 70,
    so 40 + 30 = ______

11. 10 + 40 = 50,
    so 40 + 10 = ______

12. 20 + 50 = 70,
    so 50 + 20 = ______

HOME ACTIVITY • Put out 3 dimes and 4 dimes. Remind your child that each dime is worth 10 cents. Ask your child to add 3 + 4 and then 30 + 40. Repeat with other groups of dimes.

Name ______________________

Count On Tens and Ones

What is 56 + 2?

Say 56.
Count on by ones.

Think

56 57, 58

56 + 2 = 58

What is 56 + 20?

Say 56.
Count on by tens.

Think

56 66, 76

56 + 20 = 76

Count on to add.

1 65 + 3 = ____ 65 + 30 = ____	**2** 2 + 22 = ____ 20 + 22 = ____	**3** 47 + 2 = ____ 47 + 20 = ____
4 1 + 82 = ____ 10 + 82 = ____	**5** 2 + 62 = ____ 20 + 62 = ____	**6** 51 + 3 = ____ 51 + 30 = ____
7 3 + 27 = ____ 30 + 27 = ____	**8** 41 + 2 = ____ 41 + 20 = ____	**9** 63 + 1 = ____ 63 + 10 = ____

Talk About It ■ **Reasoning**

Look at the problem 13 + 20. Is it easier to count on from 13 or 20? Why?

Practice

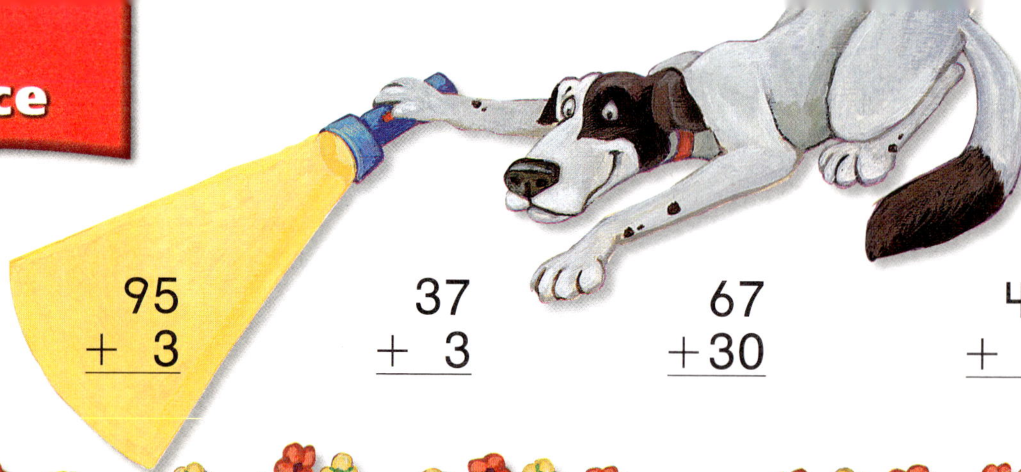

Count on to add.

1	20 + 39 59	95 + 3	37 + 3	67 + 30	43 + 2
2	1 + 39	75 + 10	29 + 10	52 + 2	84 + 10
3	20 + 32	3 + 48	49 + 2	92 + 1	38 + 30
4	75 + 2	27 + 20	88 + 1	61 + 3	30 + 59

Problem Solving ■ Number Sense

Use the number line to count on.

50 51 52 53 54 55 56 57 58 59 60 61 62

5. 51 + 10 = _____ 3 + 58 = _____ 53 + 2 = _____

HOME ACTIVITY • Ask your child to count on to add 47 + 3. Then pick any 2-digit number and have your child count on 1, 2, 3 and 10, 20, 30. Repeat several times with different starting numbers.

Name ____________________

Model Adding 1 Digit to 2 Digits

Hands On

When there are 10 or more ones, **regroup** 10 ones as 1 ten.

Show 15 + 8.

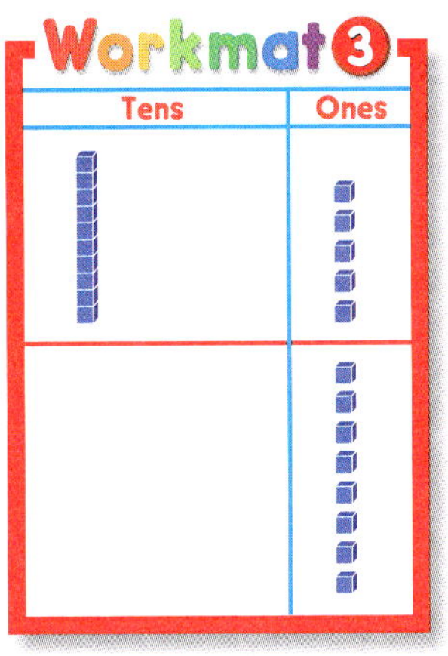

Add the ones.
5 + 8 = 13

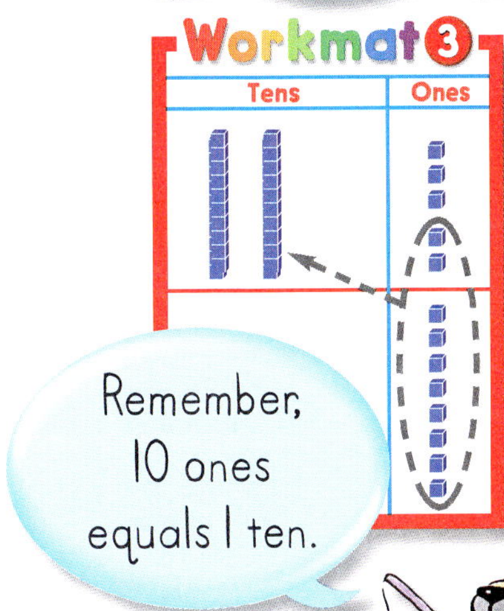

Write how many tens and ones.

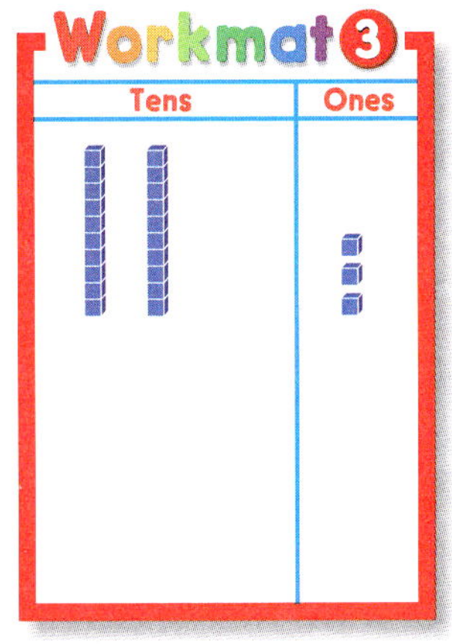

2 tens 3 ones

Use Workmat 3 and ▭ ▫.

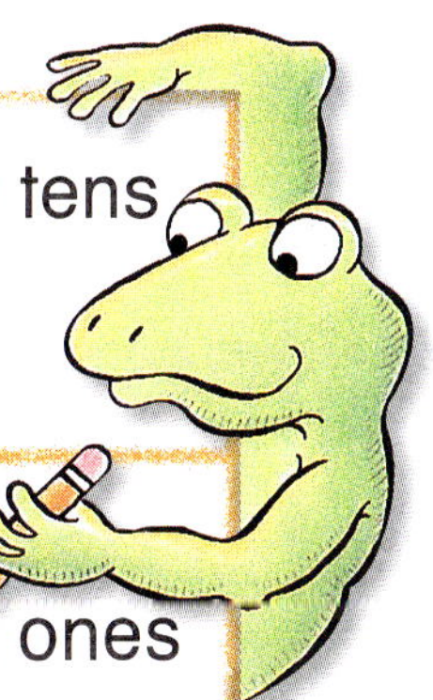

Show.	Add the ones. Are there 10 or more ones? If so, regroup 10 ones as 1 ten.	Write how many tens and ones.
1 15 + 6	(Yes) No	2 tens 1 ones
2 26 + 9	Yes No	____ tens ____ ones
3 31 + 4	Yes No	____ tens ____ ones
4 25 + 5	Yes No	____ tens ____ ones

Talk About It ▪ Reasoning

In which problems did you regroup 10 ones for 1 ten?
Use ▭ ▫ to explain why.

Practice

Use Workmat 3 and  .

Show.	Add the ones. Are there 10 or more ones? If so, regroup 10 ones as 1 ten.	Write how many tens and ones.
1. 18 + 7	(Yes) No	2 tens 5 ones
2. 25 + 8	Yes No	____ tens ____ ones
3. 32 + 4	Yes No	____ tens ____ ones
4. 47 + 4	Yes No	____ tens ____ ones
5. 35 + 5	Yes No	____ tens ____ ones
6. 16 + 7	Yes No	____ tens ____ ones

Mixed Review

Write the time.

7. 

____ : ____

8. 

____ : ____

9. 

____ : ____

HOME ACTIVITY • Ask your child to point out the problems on this page in which he or she regrouped. For each, ask why.

Name ______________________________

Model 2-Digit Addition

Hands On

When there are 10 or more ones, regroup 10 ones as 1 ten.

Show 13 + 18.

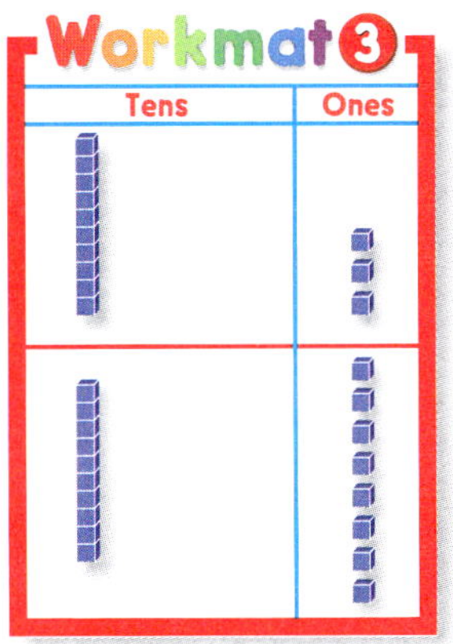

Add the ones.
3 + 8 = 11

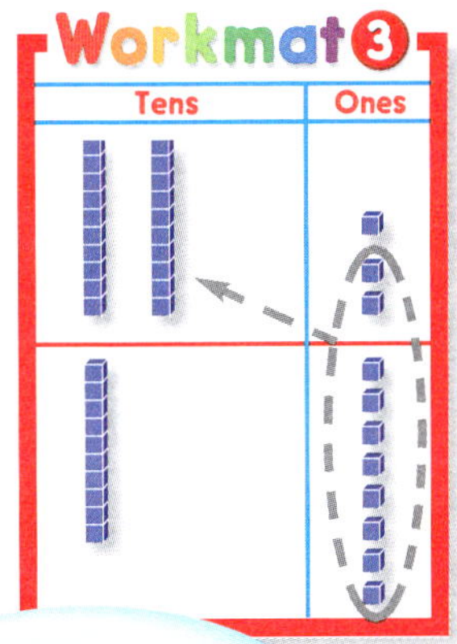

Remember, 10 ones equals 1 ten.

Write how many tens and ones.

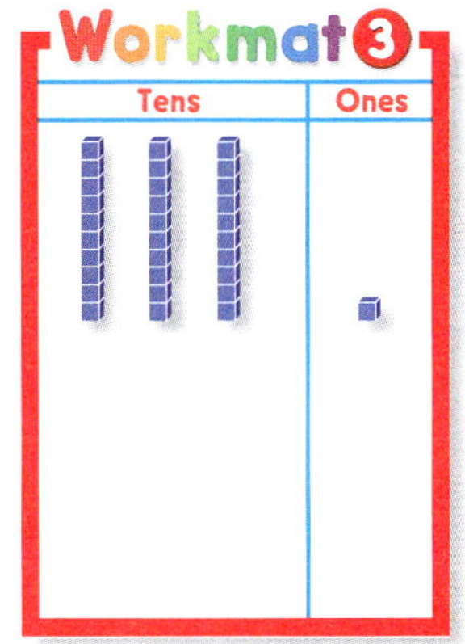

3 tens 1 one

Use Workmat 3 and tens and ones blocks.

Show.	Add the ones. Are there 10 or more ones? If so, regroup 10 ones as 1 ten.	Write how many tens and ones.
1 13 + 14	Yes (No)	2 tens 7 ones
2 13 + 17	Yes No	____ tens ____ ones
3 13 + 19	Yes No	____ tens ____ ones
4 13 + 16	Yes No	____ tens ____ ones

Talk About It ■ **Reasoning**

What would happen if you added the tens first in this problem? Could you get the correct answer? How would you do it?

$$\begin{array}{r} 13 \\ +\,18 \\ \hline \end{array}$$

Practice

Use Workmat 3 and [tens] [ones].

Show.	Add the ones. Are there 10 or more ones? If so, regroup 10 ones as 1 ten.	Write how many tens and ones.
1 59 + 16	(Yes) No	7 tens 5 ones
2 24 + 23	Yes No	____ tens ____ ones
3 62 + 28	Yes No	____ tens ____ ones
4 17 + 16	Yes No	____ tens ____ ones
5 33 + 55	Yes No	____ tens ____ ones
6 13 + 15	Yes No	____ tens ____ ones

Problem Solving ■ Reasoning

Three children got different answers when they did this problem. Circle the correct answer. Explain the mistakes you think the other two children made.

7

$$\begin{array}{r} 47 \\ +25 \\ \hline \end{array}$$

22	72	612

HOME ACTIVITY • Ask your child to tell why he or she grouped some of the problems on this page and not others.

Name ______________________________

UNDERSTAND › PLAN › SOLVE › CHECK

Problem Solving
Make a Model

There are 27 children playing kickball on a playground. Then 13 children join the game. How many children in all are playing kickball?

UNDERSTAND

What do you want to find out?

PLAN

You can make a model to solve the problem.

SOLVE

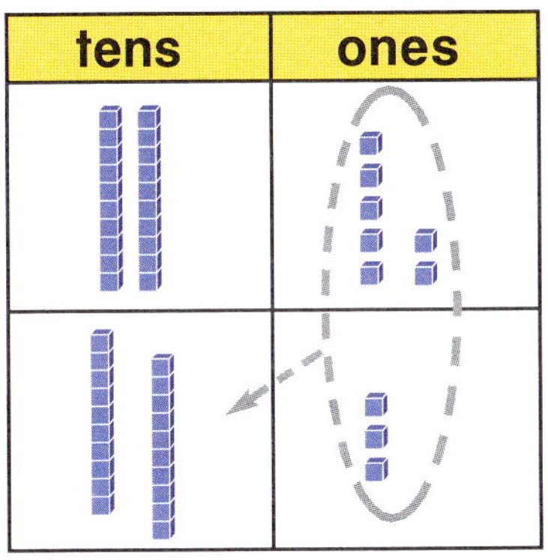

tens	ones
1	
2	7
+ 1	3
4	0

40 children

CHECK

Does your answer make sense? Explain.

Use Workmat 3 and tens and ones blocks.
Add. Regroup if you need to.
Write the sum.

1. At 12:00 in the lunchroom, there are 39 girls and 34 boys. How many children are eating lunch at 12:00?

_______ children

tens	ones
1	
3	9
+ 3	4

2. In Ms. Dodge's class, 7 boys and 15 girls bring their lunch to school. How many children bring their lunch?

_______ children

tens	ones
1	
	7
+ 1	5

Practice

Use Workmat 3 and tens and ones blocks.
Add. Regroup if you need to.
Write the sum.

1 There are 10 boys and 12 girls playing soccer on the field. How many children are playing soccer?

22 children

	tens	ones
	1	0
+	1	2
	2	2

2 The Red Team scores 13 goals on Monday and 8 on Tuesday. How many goals does the team score in all?

_______ goals

	tens	ones
+		

3 The soccer players eat 12 cheese pizzas and 9 sausage pizzas. How many pizzas do they eat?

_______ pizzas

	tens	ones
+		

4 At the soccer party there are 29 blue balloons and 37 red balloons. How many balloons are there in all?

_______ balloons

	tens	ones
+		

Math Journal

Write About It

Write a story about adding two numbers.
Both numbers are between 0 and 40.

HOME ACTIVITY • Make up a problem like the ones on this page. Have your child use pennies and dimes (see page 156) to solve the problem.

Name ____________________________

Review/Test
Chapter 11

CHECK ■ Concepts and Skills

Add.

1

$$\begin{array}{r} 2 \\ +3 \\ \hline \end{array} \qquad \begin{array}{r} 2 \text{ tens} \\ +3 \text{ tens} \\ \hline \text{tens} \end{array} \qquad \begin{array}{r} 20 \\ +30 \\ \hline \end{array}$$

2

$$\begin{array}{r} 4 \\ +5 \\ \hline \end{array} \qquad \begin{array}{r} 4 \text{ tens} \\ +5 \text{ tens} \\ \hline \text{tens} \end{array} \qquad \begin{array}{r} 40 \\ +50 \\ \hline \end{array}$$

3 Count on to add.

$55 + 2 =$ ______ $30 + 42 =$ ______ $47 + 10 =$ ______

Use Workmat 3 and [base-ten blocks].

Show.	Add the ones. Are there 10 or more ones? If so, regroup 10 ones as 1 ten.	Write how many tens and ones.
4 25 + 16	Yes No	____ tens ____ ones
5 46 + 19	Yes No	____ tens ____ ones

CHECK ■ Problem Solving

Use Workmat 3 and [base-ten blocks]. Add.
Regroup if you need to. Write the sum.

6 13 children went to the soccer game.
18 children went to the baseball game.
How many children in all went to a game?

______ children

tens	ones
+	

Name ______________________

Standardized Test Prep
Chapters 1–11

Choose the best answer for questions 1–5.

1

$$\begin{array}{r} 40 \\ +\,20 \\ \hline \end{array}$$

○ 6 ○ 16 ○ 50 ○ 60

2 $72 + 4 =$ ______

○ 76 ○ 80 ○ 81 ○ 112

3 Which does the model show?

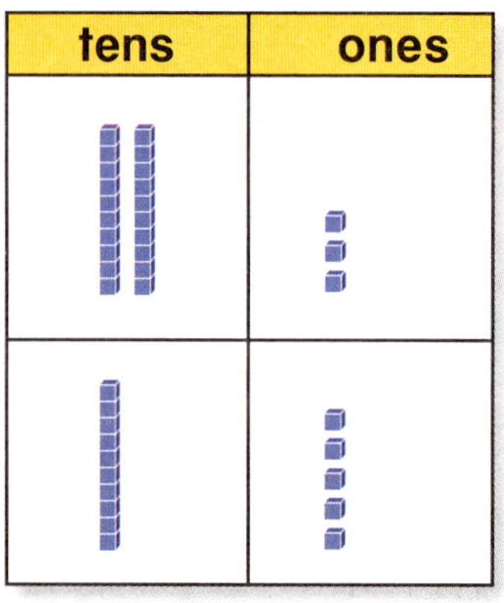

○ 33 + 15 ○ 23 + 15

○ 23 + 16 ○ 22 + 14

4 Jasmine has 64 crayons. Kelli has 12 crayons. How many crayons do they have in all?

○ 76 ○ 78 ○ 87 ○ 97

5 Which number matches the words?

sixty-four

○ 60 ○ 604 ○ 64 ○ 614

Show What You Know

6 Use red and blue. Color the tens.
Show two different ways. Write the numbers.

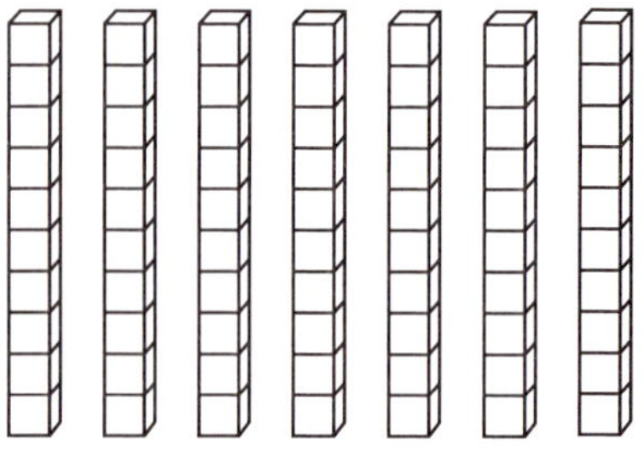

___ tens + ___ tens = ___tens

___ + ___ = ___

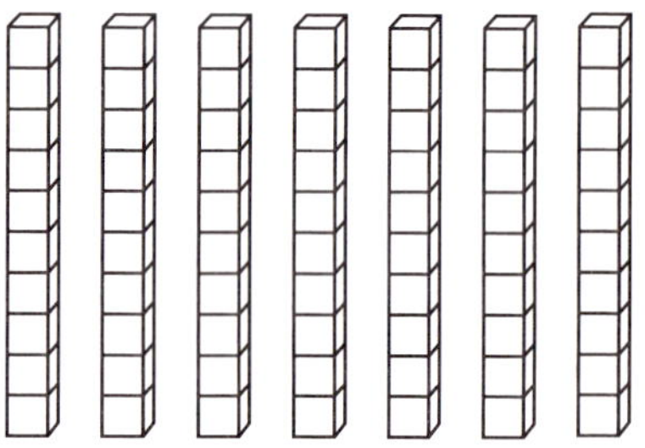

___ tens + ___ tens = ___tens

___ + ___ = ___

CHAPTER 12

2-Digit Addition

Make the addition problem that has the greatest sum.

SCHOOL HOME CONNECTION

Dear Family,

Today we started Chapter 12. We will add more 2-digit numbers and learn how to estimate. Here is the math vocabulary and an activity for us to do together at home.

Love,

____

My Math Words

estimate sums

Vocabulary

estimate sums One way to find out *about* how many in all is to estimate. You can estimate by rounding each number to the closer ten and then adding the tens.

Estimate 39 + 23 as 40 + 20.

40 + 20 = 60

So 39 + 23 is about 60.

Visit *The Learning Site* for additional ideas and activities. www.harcourtschool.com

ACTIVITY

Give your child jars, cans, and boxes that contain up to 48 ounces of food. Ask your child to choose two of the items and add the ounces to find the total.

Books to Share

To read about addition with your child, look for these books in your local library.

17 Kings and 42 Elephants,
by Margaret Mahy,
Dial Books, 1990.

Pancakes, Pancakes,
by Eric Carle,
Aladdin, 1998.

E I E I O,
by Gus Clarke,
Lothrop, Lee & Shepard, 1993.

Name ______________________

Add 2-Digit Numbers

Hands On

24 + 18 = ____

Step 1

Add the ones.
4 + 8 = 12.

tens	ones
☐	
2	4
+ 1	8

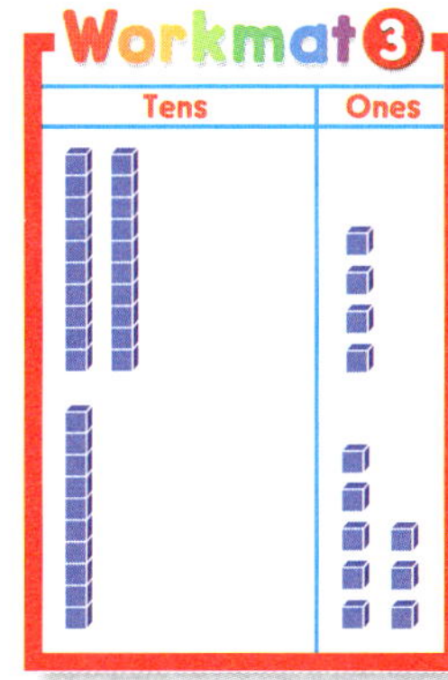

Step 2

Regroup 12 ones to make 1 ten and 2 ones. Write 1 to show the new ten.

tens	ones
1	
2	4
+ 1	8
	2

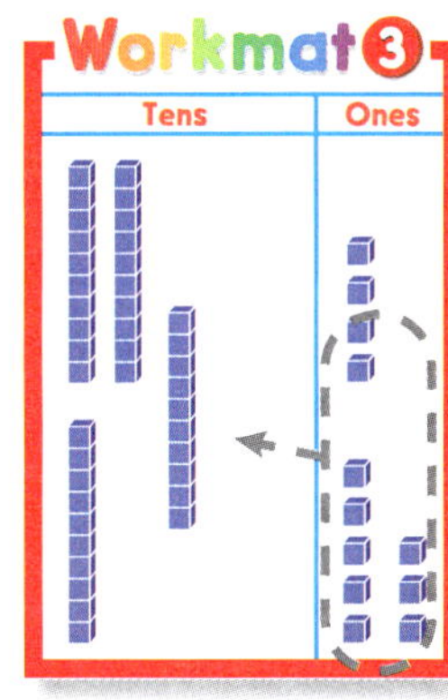

Step 3

Add the tens.
Write how many.

tens	ones
1	
2	4
+ 1	8
4	2

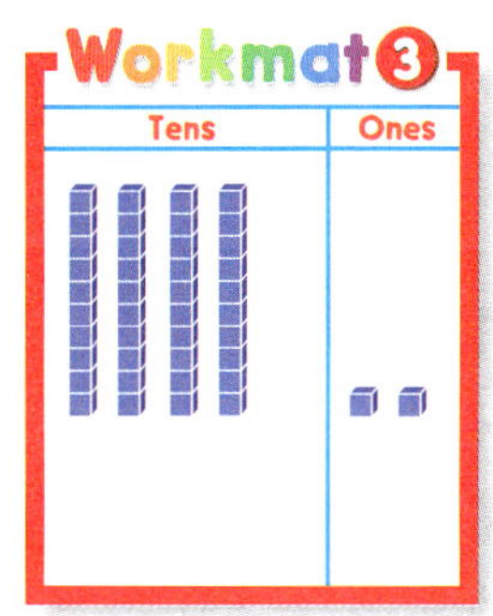

Use Workmat 3 and [tens block] [ones cube].
Add. Regroup if you need to.

1

tens	ones
☐	
2	7
+ 3	9

2

tens	ones
☐	
4	6
+	8

3

tens	ones
☐	
5	4
+ 1	6

4

tens	ones
☐	
3	5
+ 4	4

Talk About It ■ **Reasoning**

How can you tell if you need to regroup in an addition problem?

Practice

Use Workmat 3 and [tens blocks] [ones block].
Add. Regroup if you need to.

1

tens	ones
1	
5	7
+	5
6	2

2

tens	ones
☐	
4	7
+3	6

3

tens	ones
☐	
2	3
+5	8

4

tens	ones
☐	
7	9
+1	3

5

tens	ones
☐	
4	1
+2	9

6

tens	ones
☐	
	9
+5	6

7

tens	ones
☐	
1	3
+5	5

8

tens	ones
☐	
8	3
+	7

9

tens	ones
☐	
3	6
+	5

10

tens	ones
☐	
6	5
+1	8

11

tens	ones
☐	
2	2
+2	6

12

tens	ones
☐	
4	9
+4	2

Problem Solving • Application

Use Workmat 3 and [tens blocks] [ones block]. Solve.

13 The Empire State Building has 6 elevators for packages. It has 67 elevators for people. How many elevators are there in all?

_______ elevators

14 On the elevator, it takes 45 seconds to ride to the 86th floor. It takes 12 seconds more to ride to the 102nd floor. How long does it take to ride to the 102nd floor?

_______ seconds

HOME ACTIVITY • Have your child use small objects to add two 2-digit numbers.

Name ______________________

More 2-Digit Addition

$12 + 18 =$ ______

Step 1

Add the ones.
$2 + 8 = 10$.
Do you need to regroup?

Yes No

tens	ones
☐	
1	2
+ 1	8

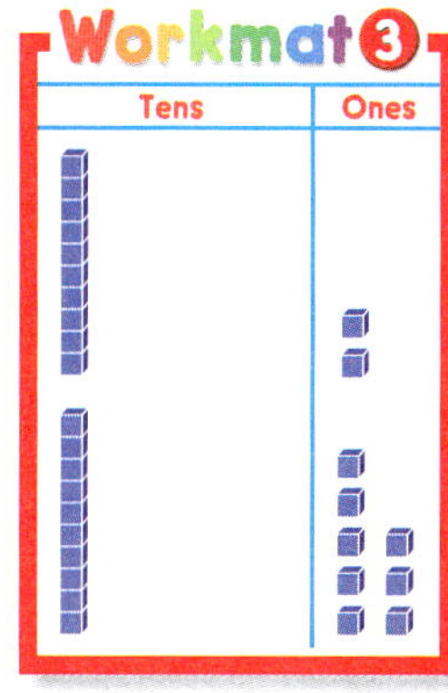

Step 2

Regroup if you need to.
Write how many.

tens	ones
1	
1	2
+ 1	8
	0

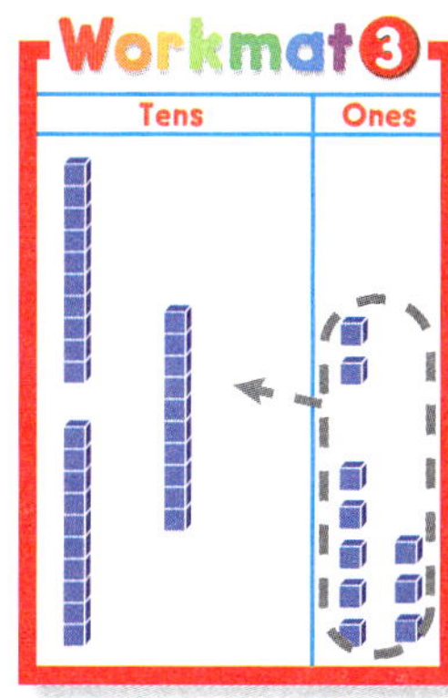

Step 3

Add the tens.

tens	ones
1	
1	2
+ 1	8
3	0

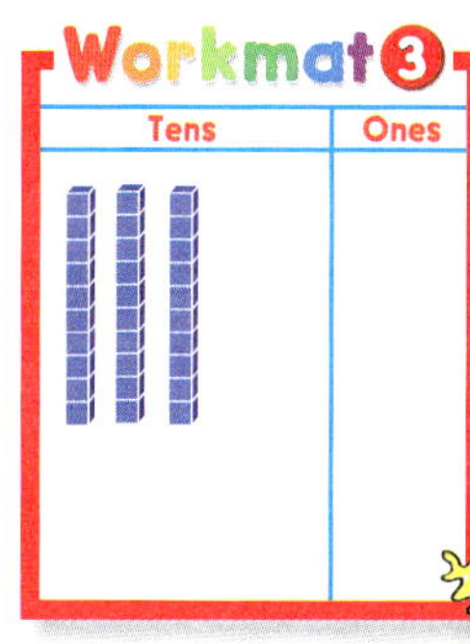

Use Workmat 3 and 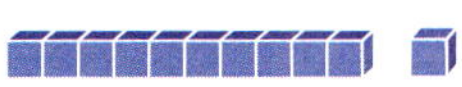 .
Add. Regroup if you need to.

1

tens	ones
☐	
2	3
+ 2	9

2

tens	ones
☐	
2	1
+ 1	9

3

tens	ones
☐	
4	2
+ 3	2

4

tens	ones
☐	
6	7
+ 2	5

Talk About It ■ **Reasoning**

Why is this answer wrong?

Practice

Use Workmat 3 and [tens and ones blocks].
Add. Regroup if you need to.

1

tens	ones
1	
3	7
+3	3
7	0

2

tens	ones
☐	
4	8
+3	5

3

tens	ones
☐	
5	4
+2	7

4

tens	ones
☐	
7	2
+1	7

5

tens	ones
☐	
7	2
+1	4

6

tens	ones
☐	
5	3
+1	9

7

tens	ones
☐	
3	7
+5	6

8

tens	ones
☐	
3	4
+3	6

9

tens	ones
☐	
2	8
+3	5

10

tens	ones
☐	
5	8
+2	4

11

tens	ones
☐	
2	3
+4	6

12

tens	ones
☐	
2	4
+3	9

Mixed Review

Write the number.

13 6 tens 4 ones = ______

14 3 tens 9 ones = ______

15 5 tens 0 ones = ______

16 7 tens 2 ones = ______

HOME ACTIVITY • Show your child a problem such as 17+14= ____. Ask whether it will be necessary to regroup and how he or she knows.

Name ______________________

Rewrite 2-Digit Addition

58 + 19 = ____

tens	ones
1	
5	8
+ 1	9
7	7

Rewrite the numbers in each problem.
Then add.

1 37 + 33

tens	ones
☐	
+	

2 48 + 36

tens	ones
☐	
+	

3 54 + 27

tens	ones
☐	
+	

4 62 + 6

tens	ones
☐	
+	

5 53 + 19

tens	ones
☐	
+	

6 8 + 65

tens	ones
☐	
+	

7 36 + 57

tens	ones
☐	
+	

8 28 + 43

tens	ones
☐	
+	

Talk About It ■ **Reasoning**

John added 54 + 7. He got a sum of 124. What did John do wrong?

Practice

Rewrite the numbers in each problem.
Then add.

1. 23 + 29

tens	ones
1	
2	3
+ 2	9
5	2

2. 51 + 17

tens	ones
+	

3. 42 + 9

tens	ones
+	

4. 67 + 28

tens	ones
+	

5. 25 + 56

tens	ones
+	

6. 14 + 38

tens	ones
+	

7. 66 + 7

tens	ones
+	

8. 80 + 18

tens	ones
+	

9. 5 + 37

tens	ones
+	

10. 42 + 15

tens	ones
+	

11. 70 + 17

tens	ones
+	

12. 22 + 22

tens	ones
+	

Mixed Review

Write even or odd.

13. 47 ______

14. 56 ______

15. 19 ______

HOME ACTIVITY • Say a 2-digit addition problem with a sum of 99 or less. Have your child write the problem and then add to solve. Repeat several times.

Name ______________________________

UNDERSTAND › PLAN › SOLVE › CHECK

Problem Solving
Estimate Sums

Carol saw 36 rain forest animals in the zoo. Charles saw 33 in a nature show. About how many rain forest animals did they see in all?

You **estimate** when you don't need an exact answer.

UNDERSTAND

What do you want to find out?

PLAN

You can estimate sums to solve the problem.

SOLVE

You can **round** numbers when you want to know about how many. When you round a number to the nearest ten, you can find the ten it is closer to on a number line.

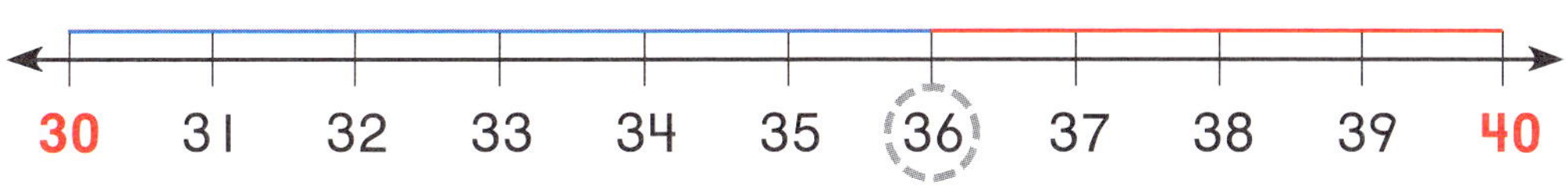

Circle 36 on the number line. 36 is closer to 40 than to 30.

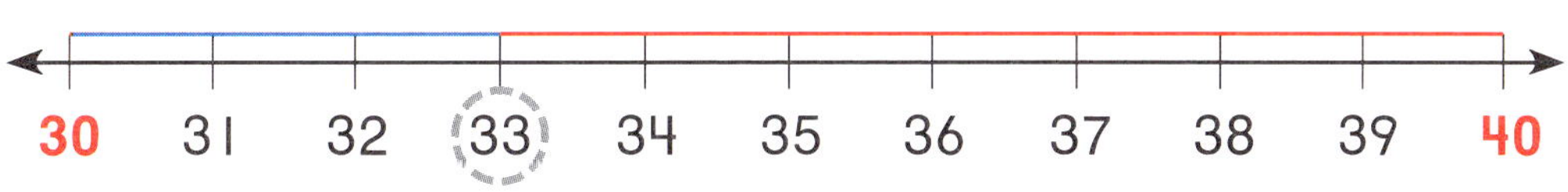

Circle 33 on the number line. 33 is closer to 30 than to 40.

Now, add your rounded numbers.

estimate
40 + 30 70

CHECK

Does your answer make sense? Explain.

When a number is halfway between 2 tens, round to the greater ten. You would round 15 to 20. Look at the number line. Which numbers would you round to 40?

Practice

10 11 12 13 14 15 16 17 18 19 **20** 21 22 23 24 25 26 27 28 29 **30**

Use the number line to help you round.
Show your addition problem.

estimate

1. Ian has 11 buttons. Erika gives him 17 buttons. About how many buttons does Ian have now?

   about 30 buttons

   $$\begin{array}{r} 10 \\ +\ 20 \\ \hline 30 \end{array}$$

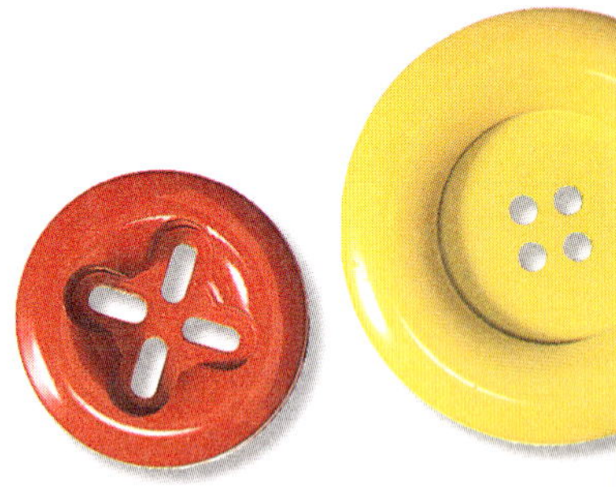

2. Greg has 26 shells. He finds 21 more shells. About how many shells does Greg have in all?

   about _______ shells

3. Bob has 19 stickers. Linda gives him 18 stickers. About how many stickers does Bob have now?

   about _______ stickers

4. Pat earned 25¢ on Monday. She earned the same amount on Tuesday. Can she buy some marbles for 40¢?

   ____

Math Journal

Write About It

Write a story about animals.
Add two numbers in your story.
Each number should be less than 50.

HOME ACTIVITY • Have your child practice estimating sums while you are at the supermarket. Pick two items with prices of up to 49¢. Ask your child to estimate the total price.

Name ______________________________

Review/Test
Chapter 12

CHECK ■ Concepts and Skills

Use Workmat 3 and [tens] [ones].
Add. Regroup if you need to.

1

tens	ones
□	
2	6
+	7

2

tens	ones
□	
4	9
+	9

3

tens	ones
□	
2	4
+ 1	8

4

tens	ones
□	
4	3
+ 3	8

Use Workmat 3 and [tens] [ones].
Add. Regroup if you need to.

5

tens	ones
□	
2	7
+ 5	2

6

tens	ones
□	
3	8
+ 4	4

Rewrite the numbers in each problem.
Then add.

7 32 + 27

tens	ones
□	
+	

8 74 + 8

tens	ones
□	
+	

CHECK ■ Problem Solving

Use the number line to help you round. Show your addition problem.

10 11 12 13 14 15 16 17 18 19 **20** 21 22 23 24 25 26 27 28 29 **30**

9 Lee has 17 sports cards. Mike gives her 19 more cards. About how many sports cards does Lee have now?

about ______ sports cards

estimate

Name ________________________

Standardized Test Prep
Chapters 1–12

Choose the best answer for questions 1–4.

1 Which is another way to write 29 + 44 = ______?

92 + 44	24 + 94	44 + 92	29 + 44
○	○	○	○

2

tens	ones
□	
2	7
+ 1	2

15 ○ 35 ○ 39 ○ 41 ○

3

tens	ones
□	
3	7
+ 1	4

50 ○ 51 ○ 60 ○ 61 ○

4 What time does the clock show?

6:20 ○ 6:25 ○

5:20 ○ 5:25 ○

Show What You Know

5 What numbers can you add to 56 without regrouping?
Write the numbers. Write the sums.

tens	ones
5	6
+	

tens	ones
5	6
+	

tens	ones
5	6
+	

tens	ones
5	6
+	

CHAPTER 13

Practice 2-Digit Addition

SCHOOL HOME CONNECTION

Dear Family,

Today we started Chapter 13. We will practice adding 2-digit numbers and use mental math to solve problems. Here is the math vocabulary and an activity for us to do together at home.

Love,

____

My Math Words

mental math

Vocabulary

mental math A way to solve problems without using a pencil or paper.

$$\begin{array}{r} 64 \\ +\ 25 \\ \hline \end{array}$$

Add the tens. $\begin{array}{r} 60 \\ +\ 20 \\ \hline 80 \end{array}$

Add the ones. $\begin{array}{r} 4 \\ +\ 5 \\ \hline 9 \end{array}$

Find the sum. $\begin{array}{r} 80 \\ +\ 9 \\ \hline 89 \end{array}$

Visit ***The Learning Site*** **for additional ideas and activities.**
www.harcourtschool.com

ACTIVITY

Give your child a grocery receipt or ad from the newspaper. Have him or her find two items that each cost less than 50 cents and add their prices.

Books to Share

To read about addition with your child, look for these books in your local library.

The Hundred Penny Box,
by Sharon Bell Mathis,
Viking, 1975.

The Philharmonic Gets Dressed,
by Karla Kuskin,
HarperCollins, 1986.

Baseball's Greatest Hitters,
by S. A. Kramer,
Random House, 2000.

Name ______________________________

More 2-Digit Addition

There were 35 cranes and 29 pelicans drinking water at the pond. How many cranes and pelicans were at the pond in all?

Step 1

Add the ones.
5 + 9 = 14.

tens	ones
3	5
+2	9

Step 2

Regroup if you need to.

tens	ones
1	
3	5
+2	9
	4

Step 3

Add the tens.

tens	ones
1	
3	5
+2	9
6	4

There were __64__ cranes and pelicans.

Add.

1

tens	ones
2	6
+2	7

tens	ones
5	3
+1	7

tens	ones
4	7
+2	1

tens	ones
3	9
+	7

2

tens	ones
1	8
+4	4

tens	ones
3	2
+2	8

tens	ones
6	5
+1	5

tens	ones
4	6
+1	3

Talk About It ▪ Reasoning

How do you know when to regroup the ones?

Practice

Add.

1

tens	ones
2	3
+ 1	7
4	0

tens	ones
1	3
+ 1	2

tens	ones
3	2
+ 2	9

tens	ones
5	1
+ 1	2

2

tens	ones
3	7
+ 4	4

tens	ones
4	9
+	7

tens	ones
5	6
+ 2	7

tens	ones
6	6
+ 1	6

3

tens	ones
3	5
+ 2	4

tens	ones
2	8
+ 2	3

tens	ones
	9
+ 3	6

tens	ones
3	8
+ 1	5

Problem Solving ■ Application

Solve each clue.
Use the answers to complete the puzzle.

Across
1. 40 doubled
2. 10 more than 20
3. 2 more than 39
4. 2 less than 80
5. 1 less than 50

Down
1. 60 + 20
3. 2 less than 50
4. 5 more than 70
5. 20 doubled

1.		■	■	2.	
	■	3.		■	■
■	4.		■	5.	
■		■			■

HOME ACTIVITY • Have your child pick any two numbers from the calendar and add them. Repeat with other numbers.

Name ______________________________

Use Mental Math to Find Sums

Janie saw 43 blue birds.
She saw 25 red birds.
How many birds did she see altogether?

Here is a way to add 43 + 25 in your head.
Adding in your head is called **mental math**.

Think.
Add the tens.
40 + 20 = 60
Add the ones.
3 + 5 = 8
Then add the sums.
60 + 8 = 68

Janie saw 68 birds.

Use mental math to add.

1 19 + 21 = 40

Think

10 + 20 = 30

9 + 1 = 10

30 + 10 = 40

2 33 + 56 = ____

Think

____ + ____ = ____

____ + ____ = ____

____ + ____ = ____

3 41 + 26 = ____

Think

____ + ____ = ____

____ + ____ = ____

____ + ____ = ____

4 35 + 25 = ____

Think

____ + ____ = ____

____ + ____ = ____

____ + ____ = ____

Talk About It ■ Reasoning

If you think 20 + 40 = 60 and 7 + 3 = 10, what two numbers are you adding?

Practice

Use mental math to add.

33 + 59 = ___?___

Think.
Add the tens. **30 + 50 = 80**
Then add the ones. **3 + 9 = 12**
Add the sums. **80 + 12 = 92**

33 + 59 = 92

1. 45 + 13 = ______

Think

______ + ______ = ______
______ + ______ = ______
______ + ______ = ______

2. 52 + 42 = ______

Think

______ + ______ = ______
______ + ______ = ______
______ + ______ = ______

3. 61 + 29 = ______

Think

______ + ______ = ______
______ + ______ = ______
______ + ______ = ______

Problem Solving ■ Mental Math

Use mental math. Is the sum correct?
Circle Yes or No. Then write the correct sum.

4. 39 + 49 = 88

Yes No ______

5. 67 + 24 = 81

Yes No ______

HOME ACTIVITY • Have your child tell how he or she added the numbers for the exercises on this page.

Name ______________________________

Practice Adding 2-Digit Numbers

Circle the problems in which you will need to regroup. Then add.

1

28	11	14	54	37
+ 47	+ 56	+ 28	+ 9	+ 36
75				

2

35	14	42	16	63
+ 29	+ 17	+ 36	+ 39	+ 4

3

26	73	54	49	21
+ 19	+ 24	+ 9	+ 18	+ 12

4

57	39	26
+ 17	+ 37	+ 36

5

48	35	61
+ 22	+ 49	+ 17

Talk About It ■ **Reasoning**

How did you know which problems to circle?

Practice

Circle the problems in which you will need to regroup. Then add.

1

13	25	67	19	73
+ 39	+ 8	+ 20	+ 48	+ 13
52				

2

17	33	19	14	73
+ 46	+ 3	+ 24	+ 28	+ 19

3

41	73	42	35	71
+ 25	+ 9	+ 39	+ 20	+ 19

4

25	29	47	79	17
+ 37	+ 41	+ 25	+ 3	+ 15

Problem Solving ■ Estimation

5 You want a sum of about 60. Which 2 numbers would you add?

_____ _____

6 You want a sum of about 90. Which 2 numbers would you add?

_____ _____

28
47
59
8

HOME ACTIVITY • Have your child tell you how to add 2-digit numbers. Together, make up addition problems using the digits from your phone number. The sums should be 99 or less.

Name ____________________

UNDERSTAND › PLAN › SOLVE › CHECK

Problem Solving
Make and Use a Graph

Some children at school are building birdhouses for a project. Use the chart to answer the questions.

Birdhouses Made	
Kindergarten	7
First Grade	10
Second Grade	14
Third Grade	13

1. How many birdhouses in all did kindergarten and third grade make? 20

2. How many birdhouses in all did second and third grade make? ______

3. Use the chart to complete the graph.

Birdhouses Made

Kindergarten															
First Grade															
Second Grade															
Third Grade															
	0	1	2	3	4	5	6	7	8	9	10	11	12	13	14 15

Use the graph to answer the questions.

4. How many birdhouses in all were made? ______

5. How many more birdhouses did second grade make than first grade? ______

6. How many more birdhouses would kindergarten need to make to equal the number made by second grade? ______

Practice

For a science project, three second-grade classes decided to learn about jungle animals.

1 How many children in all learned about gorillas and crocodiles?

32 children

2 How many children in all learned about elephants and tigers?

_______ children

3 Complete the graph to show how many children learned about each animal.

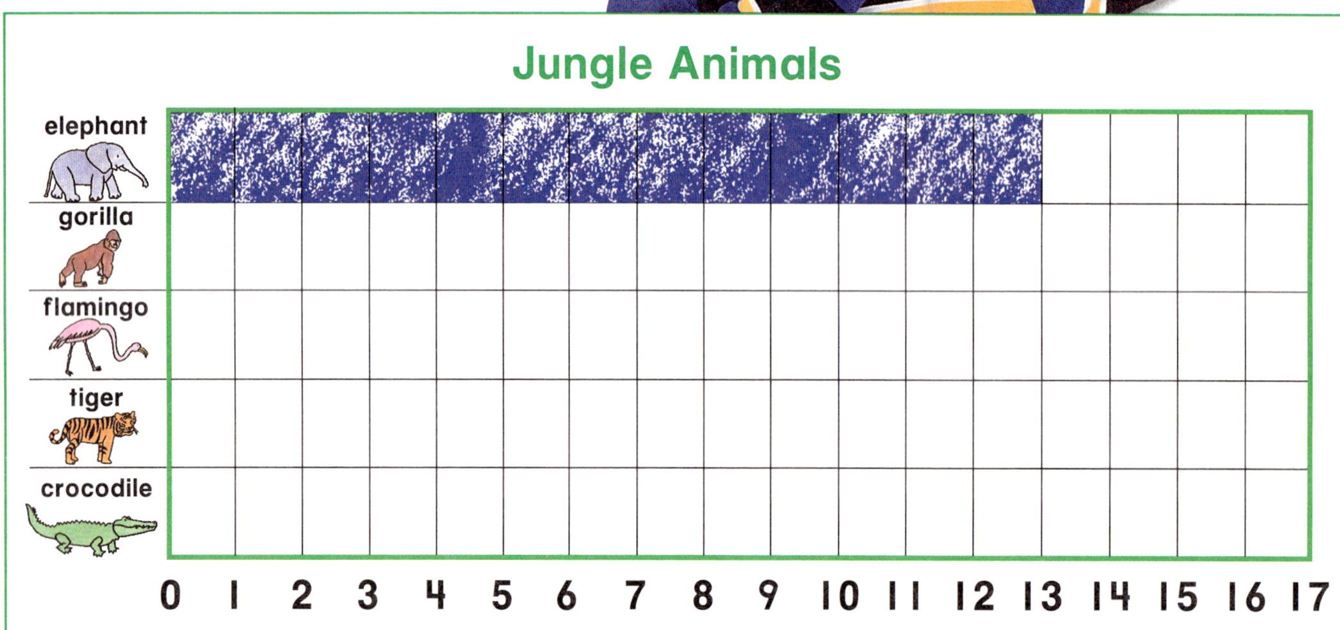

Use the graph to answer the question.

4 How many children in all learned about jungle animals? _______ children

Write About It

What questions could you ask about the graph? Write some questions of your own.

HOME ACTIVITY • Have your child write his or her own addition questions, using data from the graph.

Name ______________________________

Review/Test
Chapter 13

CHECK ■ Concepts and Skills

Add.

1

tens	ones
1	6
+2	3

2

tens	ones
6	4
+1	7

Use mental math to add.

3 41 + 18 =

Think

____ + ____ = ____

____ + ____ = ____

____ + ____ = ____

Add.

4 $\begin{array}{r} 21 \\ +18 \\ \hline \end{array}$

5 $\begin{array}{r} 35 \\ +26 \\ \hline \end{array}$

6 $\begin{array}{r} 17 \\ +23 \\ \hline \end{array}$

7 $\begin{array}{r} 32 \\ +61 \\ \hline \end{array}$

8 $\begin{array}{r} 53 \\ +32 \\ \hline \end{array}$

CHECK ■ Problem Solving

9 Pat and Joe saw some birds at the park. They made a chart.

Birds	
blue jays	9
crows	10
robins	12

Complete the graph to show how many birds Pat and Joe saw.

Birds												
blue jays												
crows												
robins												
	0	1	2	3	4	5	6	7	8	9	10	11	12

10 How many more crows than blue jays did Pat and Joe see? ______

11 How many birds did Pat and Joe see altogether? ______

Name ______________________________

Standardized Test Prep
Chapters 1–13

Choose the best answer for questions 1–4 .

1

$$\begin{array}{r} 55 \\ +\ 38 \\ \hline \end{array}$$

17 ○ 18 ○ 93 ○ 94 ○

2

$$\begin{array}{r} 66 \\ +\ 23 \\ \hline \end{array}$$

89 ○ 83 ○ 49 ○ 43 ○

3 Which number tells how many children in all like sparrows or doves?

15 ○ 27 ○ 28 ○ 30 ○

4 Which is the tenth month of the year?

March ○ September ○ October ○ November ○

Show What You Know

5 Use four of these numbers.
Write them in the boxes to make each sum.

10	20	18
12	15	5

$$\begin{array}{r} \square \\ +\ \square \\ \hline 25 \end{array} \qquad \begin{array}{r} \square \\ +\ \square \\ \hline 30 \end{array}$$

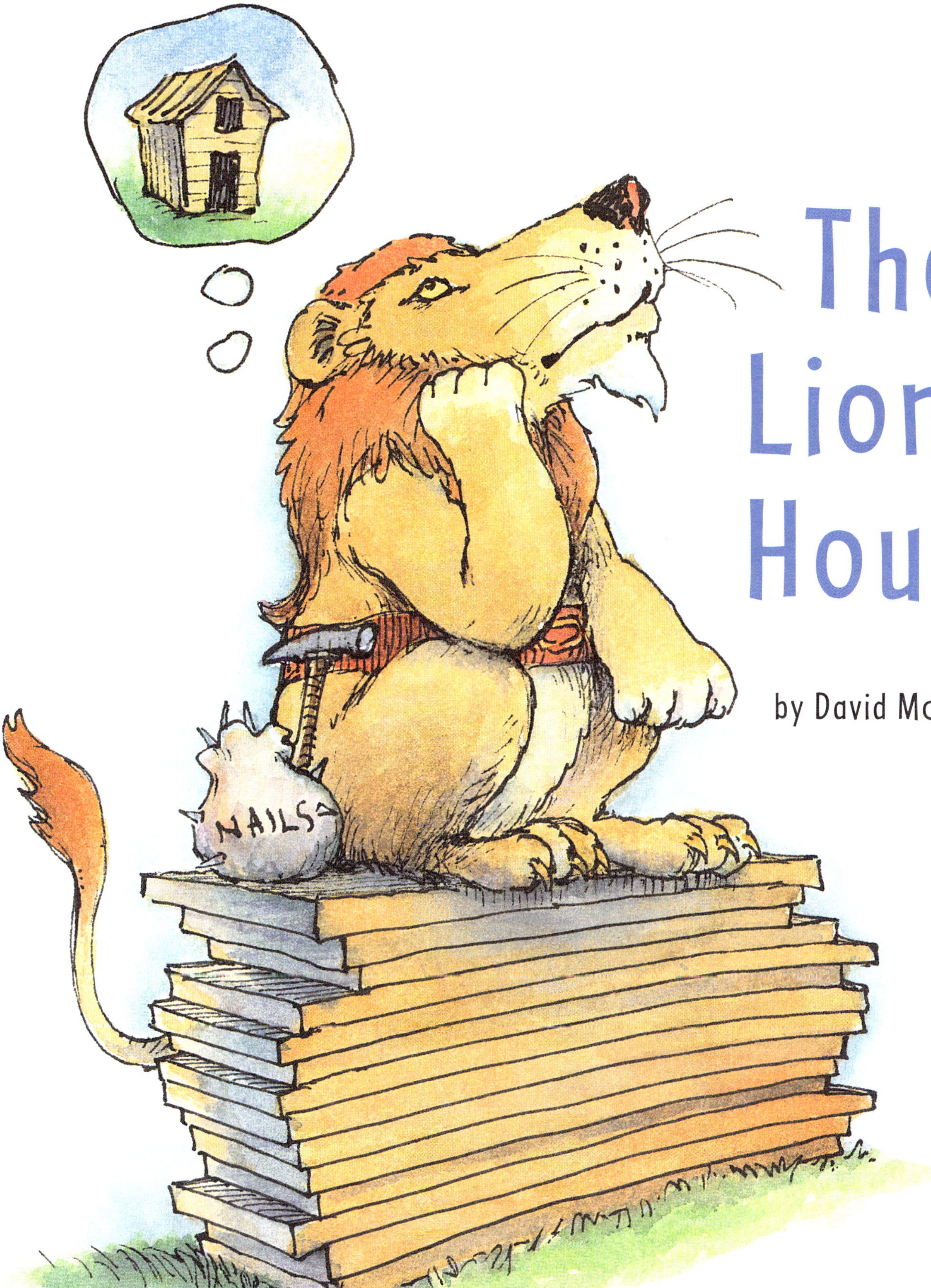

The Lion's House

by David McPhail

This book will help me review two-digit addition.

This book belongs to ______________________.

A

A lion wanted to build a house. The lion had 14 pieces of wood and 21 nails.

But 14 pieces of wood and 21 nails
was not enough to build a house.

Along came a bear. The bear wanted to build a house, too. The bear had 17 pieces of wood and 37 nails.

But even the bear's and lion's wood and nails together were not enough to build a house.

A rabbit came by pulling a wagon. "I have 26 pieces of wood and 42 nails," said the rabbit. "I want to build a house."

But even the rabbit's, bear's, and lion's wood and nails together were not enough to build a house.

A sheep came by pushing a wheelbarrow. The sheep said, "I have 38 pieces of wood and 51 nails. I want to build a house."

But even the sheep's, rabbit's, bear's, and lion's wood and nails together were not enough to build a house.

A mouse drove up in a truck. "I have 41 pieces of wood and 58 nails," said the mouse. "I want to build a house."

Together the lion, the bear, the rabbit, the sheep and the mouse had enough wood and nails to build a house.

They even had some wood and nails left over.

So they made a big bed and went to sleep.

The end

CHAPTER 14

Explore 2-Digit Subtraction

Make up subtraction problems. Use mental math to solve.

SCHOOL HOME CONNECTION

Dear Family,

Today we started Chapter 14. We will look at ways to subtract 2-digit numbers. Here is the math vocabulary and an activity for us to do together at home.

Love,

____

My Math Word

difference

Vocabulary

To find the **difference**, or answer, in this subtraction problem, you must regroup. To regroup, trade 1 ten for 10 ones to make 11 ones. You can now subtract the ones and write how many are left. Subtract the tens, and write how many tens are left.

tens	ones
3	11
~~4~~	~~1~~
−2	9
1	2

Visit ***The Learning Site*** **for additional ideas and activities.**
www.harcourtschool.com

ACTIVITY

Look through the newspaper with your child to find sale prices for things you buy that cost less than a dollar. Ask your child to find the difference between the sale prices and the regular prices by subtracting.

Books to Share

To read about subtraction with your child, look for these books in your local library.

The Empty Pot,
by Demi,
Henry Holt and Company, 1990.

The Relatives Came,
by Cynthia Rylant,
Turtleback, 1993.

How Many Candles?,
by Helen Griffith,
Greenwillow, 1999.

Name ______________________

Subtract Tens

What is 50 − 20?

Knowing the subtraction facts can help you subtract tens.

5 − 2 = 3

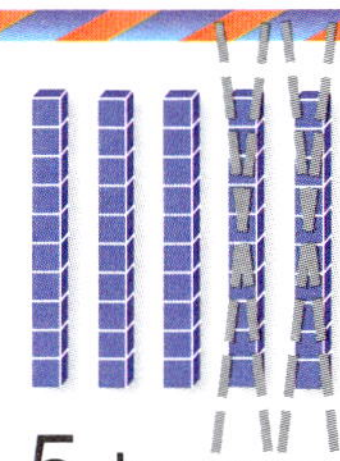

5 tens − 2 tens = 3 tens

50 − 20 = 30

Subtract.

1

6 − 1 = ______

6 tens − 1 ten = ______ tens

60 − 10 = ______

2

2 − 2 = ______

2 tens − 2 tens = ______ tens

20 − 20 = ______

3

9 − 6 = ______

9 tens   6 tens = ______ tens

90 − 60 = ______

4

7 − 5 = ______

7 tens − 5 tens = ______ tens

70 − 50 = ______

5

8 − 4 = ______

8 tens − 4 tens = ______ tens

80 − 40 = ______

6

5 − 3 = ______

5 tens − 3 tens = ______ tens

50 − 30 = ______

Talk About It ■ **Reasoning**

How does subtracting 6 tens − 2 tens help you know that 60 − 20 = 40?

Practice

Subtract.

1. $\begin{array}{r} 8 \\ -6 \\ \hline 2 \end{array}$ $\begin{array}{r} 8 \text{ tens} \\ -6 \text{ tens} \\ \hline 2 \text{ tens} \end{array}$ $\begin{array}{r} 80 \\ -60 \\ \hline 20 \end{array}$

2. $\begin{array}{r} 4 \\ -0 \\ \hline \end{array}$ $\begin{array}{r} 4 \text{ tens} \\ -0 \text{ tens} \\ \hline \text{tens} \end{array}$ $\begin{array}{r} 40 \\ -0 \\ \hline \end{array}$

3. $\begin{array}{r} 8 \\ -3 \\ \hline \end{array}$ $\begin{array}{r} 8 \text{ tens} \\ -3 \text{ tens} \\ \hline \text{tens} \end{array}$ $\begin{array}{r} 80 \\ -30 \\ \hline \end{array}$

4. $\begin{array}{r} 6 \\ -4 \\ \hline \end{array}$ $\begin{array}{r} 6 \text{ tens} \\ -4 \text{ tens} \\ \hline \text{tens} \end{array}$ $\begin{array}{r} 60 \\ -40 \\ \hline \end{array}$

5. $\begin{array}{r} 9 \\ -2 \\ \hline \end{array}$ $\begin{array}{r} 9 \text{ tens} \\ -2 \text{ tens} \\ \hline \text{tens} \end{array}$ $\begin{array}{r} 90 \\ -20 \\ \hline \end{array}$

6. $\begin{array}{r} 7 \\ -6 \\ \hline \end{array}$ $\begin{array}{r} 7 \text{ tens} \\ -6 \text{ tens} \\ \hline \text{tens} \end{array}$ $\begin{array}{r} 70 \\ -60 \\ \hline \end{array}$

7. $\begin{array}{r} 5 \\ -5 \\ \hline \end{array}$ $\begin{array}{r} 5 \text{ tens} \\ -5 \text{ tens} \\ \hline \text{tens} \end{array}$ $\begin{array}{r} 50 \\ -50 \\ \hline \end{array}$

8. $\begin{array}{r} 9 \\ -5 \\ \hline \end{array}$ $\begin{array}{r} 9 \text{ tens} \\ -5 \text{ tens} \\ \hline \text{tens} \end{array}$ $\begin{array}{r} 90 \\ -50 \\ \hline \end{array}$

Algebra

Solve.

9. $60 + 20 = 80$, so $80 - \_\_\_\_ = 60$

10. $10 + 40 = 50$, so $50 - \_\_\_\_ = 40$

11. $30 + 40 = 40 + \_\_\_\_$

12. $40 + 50 = 50 + \_\_\_\_$

HOME ACTIVITY • Put out 6 dimes. Remind your child that each dime is worth 10 cents. Ask your child to find 6 − 5 and then 60 − 50. Repeat with other groups of dimes.

Name ______________________

UNDERSTAND › PLAN › SOLVE › CHECK

Problem Solving
Choose a Method

You can choose a method to solve the problem.

You can use a calculator.

You can count back.

Say 47. Count by ones. 46, 45, 44

You can use base ten blocks.

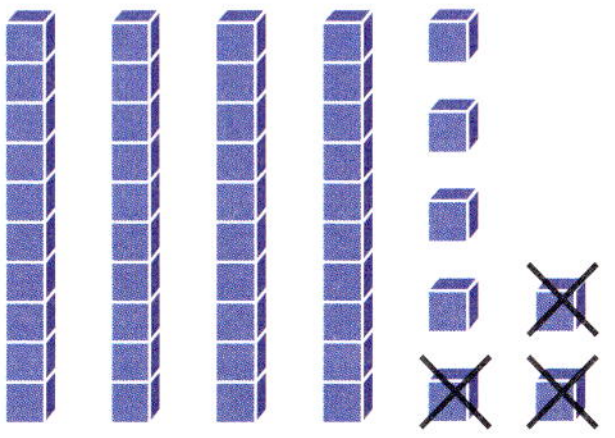

Choose a method to solve the problems.

1 65 − 3 = ____	53 − 30 = ____	78 − 20 = ____
2 92 − 1 = ____	84 − 10 = ____	42 − 2 = ____
3 56 − 10 = ____	79 − 3 = ____	14 − 10 = ____
4 16 − 3 = ____	32 − 20 = ____	20 − 3 = ____
5 53 − 1 = ____	35 − 30 = ____	81 − 2 = ____

Practice

Choose a method to solve the problems.

1	$\begin{array}{r} 84 \\ -20 \\ \hline 64 \end{array}$	$\begin{array}{r} 61 \\ -\ 3 \\ \hline \end{array}$	$\begin{array}{r} 31 \\ -10 \\ \hline \end{array}$	$\begin{array}{r} 62 \\ -30 \\ \hline \end{array}$	$\begin{array}{r} 67 \\ -\ 2 \\ \hline \end{array}$
2	$\begin{array}{r} 56 \\ -\ 1 \\ \hline \end{array}$	$\begin{array}{r} 75 \\ -10 \\ \hline \end{array}$	$\begin{array}{r} 65 \\ -\ 3 \\ \hline \end{array}$	$\begin{array}{r} 43 \\ -\ 2 \\ \hline \end{array}$	$\begin{array}{r} 75 \\ -\ 2 \\ \hline \end{array}$
3	$\begin{array}{r} 62 \\ -20 \\ \hline \end{array}$	$\begin{array}{r} 38 \\ -\ 3 \\ \hline \end{array}$	$\begin{array}{r} 46 \\ -20 \\ \hline \end{array}$	$\begin{array}{r} 59 \\ -30 \\ \hline \end{array}$	$\begin{array}{r} 94 \\ -20 \\ \hline \end{array}$
4	$\begin{array}{r} 87 \\ -30 \\ \hline \end{array}$	$\begin{array}{r} 27 \\ -20 \\ \hline \end{array}$	$\begin{array}{r} 11 \\ -\ 2 \\ \hline \end{array}$	$\begin{array}{r} 95 \\ -\ 3 \\ \hline \end{array}$	$\begin{array}{r} 89 \\ -\ 1 \\ \hline \end{array}$
5	$\begin{array}{r} 16 \\ -\ 3 \\ \hline \end{array}$	$\begin{array}{r} 47 \\ -20 \\ \hline \end{array}$	$\begin{array}{r} 51 \\ -30 \\ \hline \end{array}$	$\begin{array}{r} 63 \\ -10 \\ \hline \end{array}$	$\begin{array}{r} 56 \\ -30 \\ \hline \end{array}$

Problem Solving ■ Visual Thinking

Use the number line to count back.

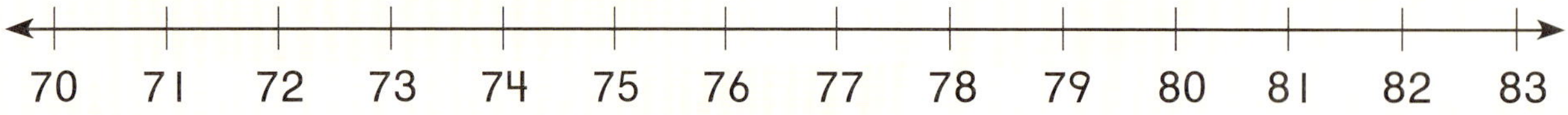

6. 82 − 1 = ______ 74 − 3 = ______ 80 − 2 = ______

HOME ACTIVITY • Ask your child to count back to subtract 69 − 3. Then pick any 2-digit number over 30 and have your child count back 1, 2, 3, 10, 20, and 30. Repeat with different starting numbers.

Name ________________________________

Regroup Tens as Ones

Hands On

Subtract 7 from 35.

$$\begin{array}{r} 35 \\ -\ \ 7 \\ \hline \end{array}$$

When there are not enough ones, break apart a ten. Regroup 1 ten as 10 ones.

Show 35. Are there enough ones to subtract 7 ones?

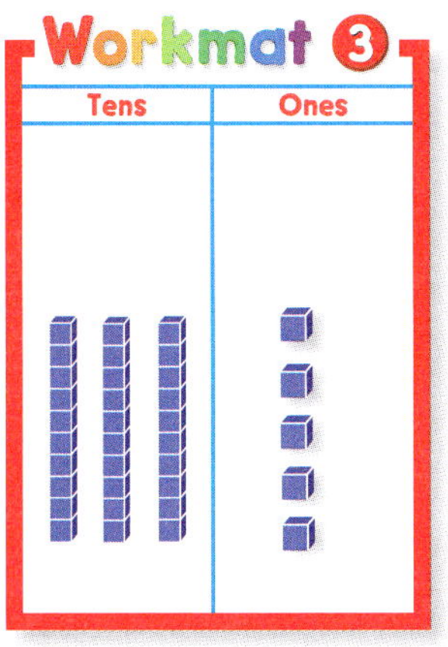

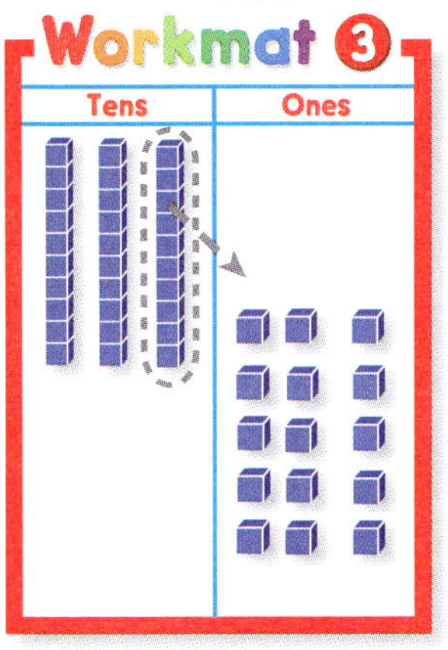

Subtract the ones. Write how many tens and ones are left.

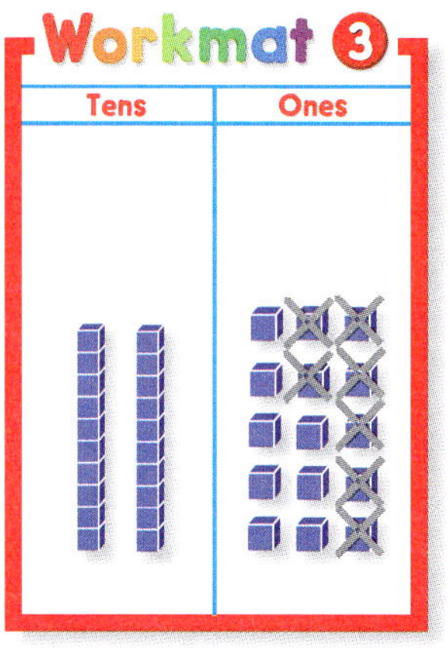

2 tens 8 ones

Use Workmat 3 and ▭ ▫.

Subtract.	Do you need to regroup?	Subtract. Write how many tens and ones are left.
1 35 − 2 = 33	Yes (No)	3 tens 3 ones
2 35 − 4 = ______	Yes No	______ tens ______ one
3 35 − 7 = ______	Yes No	______ tens ______ ones
4 35 − 8 = ______	Yes No	______ tens ______ ones

Talk About It ■ Reasoning

In which problems did you need to break apart a ten? Why?

Practice

Use Workmat 3 and .

Subtract.	Do you need to regroup?	Subtract the ones. Write how many tens and ones are left.
1 47 − 8 = 39	(Yes) No	3 tens 9 ones
2 24 − 6 = ______	Yes No	______ ten ______ ones
3 30 − 3 = ______	Yes No	______ tens ______ ones
4 26 − 5 = ______	Yes No	______ tens ______ one
5 56 − 7 = ______	Yes No	______ tens ______ ones
6 34 − 9 = ______	Yes No	______ tens ______ ones

Mixed Review

Write the total amount.

7

______¢

8

______¢

HOME ACTIVITY • Pop some popcorn, and have your child put the pieces into bags of ten, leaving some single pieces. Then have your child use the popcorn to show how to subtract a 1-digit number from a 2-digit number, for example, 8 from 32.

Name ______________________________

Model 2-Digit Subtraction

Hands On

Subtract 18 from 34.

$$\begin{array}{r} 34 \\ -\,18 \\ \hline \end{array}$$

Show 34. Are there enough ones to subtract 8 ones?

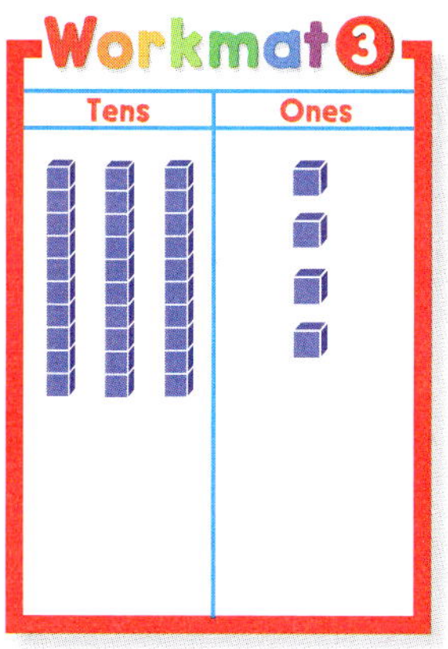

When there are not enough ones, break apart a ten. Regroup 1 ten as 10 ones.

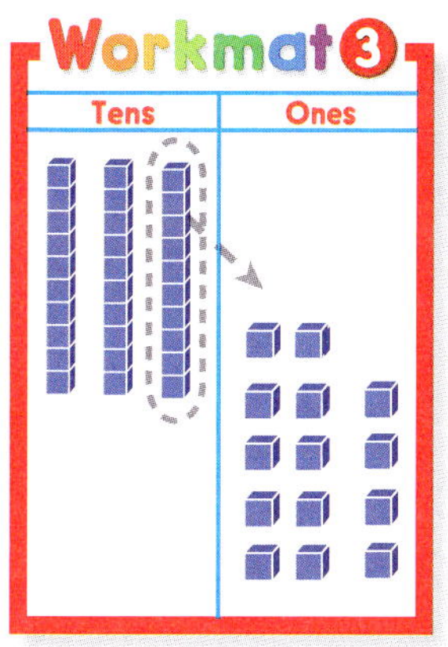

Subtract the ones. Subtract the tens. Write the difference.

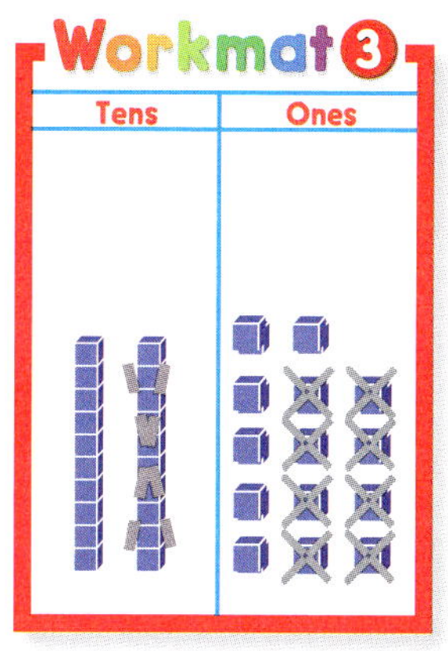

34 − 18 = 16

Use Workmat 3 and tens and ones blocks.

Subtract.	Do you need to regroup?	Subtract. Write how many are left.
1 34 − 16 = 18	(Yes) No	18
2 34 − 19 = ______	Yes No	______
3 34 − 20 = ______	Yes No	______
4 34 − 17 = ______	Yes No	______

Talk About It ■ **Reasoning**

In which problems did you need to break apart a ten? Why?

Practice

Use Workmat 3 and tens and ones blocks.

> When there are not enough ones, break apart a ten. Regroup 1 ten as 10 ones.

Subtract.	Do you need to regroup?	Subtract. Write how many are left.
1. 35 − 6 = 29	(Yes) No	29
2. 63 − 27 = ____	Yes No	____
3. 86 − 44 = ____	Yes No	____
4. 30 − 6 = ____	Yes No	____
5. 53 − 48 = ____	Yes No	____
6. 44 − 19 = ____	Yes No	____

Algebra

How many cubes are missing?

7. The total is 54. ____

8. The total is 80. ____

HOME ACTIVITY • Give your child 2 dimes and 3 pennies. Ask for 5 pennies. Have your child tell you what he or she would have to do to give you 5 pennies.

Name ______________________________

Practice Modeling 2-Digit Subtraction

Hands On

Subtract 18 from 31.

$$\begin{array}{r} 31 \\ -18 \\ \hline \end{array}$$

Show 31.

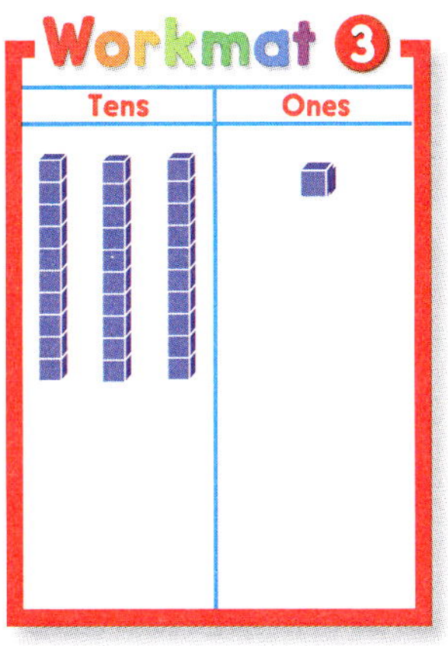

Subtract 18. Regroup if you need to.

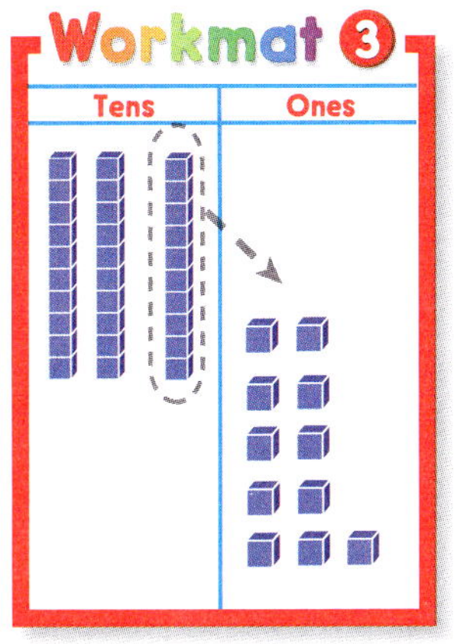

Subtract the ones.
Subtract the tens.
Write the difference.

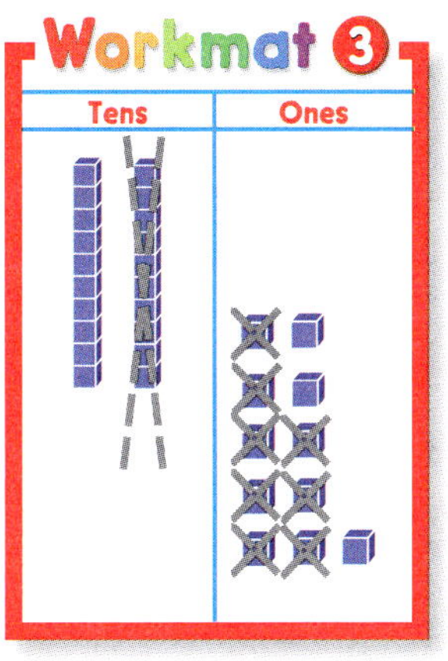

	tens	ones
	2	11
	3	1
−	1	8
	1	3

Use Workmat 3 and (tens) (ones).
Find the difference.

1

	tens	ones
	☐	☐
	4	3
−	2	7

2

	tens	ones
	☐	☐
	9	2
−		3

3

	tens	ones
	☐	☐
	7	8
−	1	5

4

	tens	ones
	☐	☐
	5	3
−	3	5

5

	tens	ones
	☐	☐
	3	0
−	1	2

6

	tens	ones
	☐	☐
	8	6
−	4	4

7

	tens	ones
	☐	☐
	5	2
−		6

8

	tens	ones
	☐	☐
	4	4
−	2	9

Talk About It ■ Reasoning

How do you know when you need to break apart a ten?

Practice

Use Workmat 3 and tens and ones blocks.
Find the difference.

1

tens	ones
1	17
2	7
− 1	8
	9

2

tens	ones
8	5
− 5	9

3

tens	ones
4	7
− 3	9

4

tens	ones
7	4
− 6	1

5

tens	ones
3	6
− 2	4

6

tens	ones
5	2
−	5

7

tens	ones
2	5
− 1	7

8

tens	ones
5	0
− 4	3

9

tens	ones
4	7
− 2	1

10

tens	ones
2	5
− 1	6

11

tens	ones
3	4
− 1	7

12

tens	ones
2	9
− 1	8

Problem Solving • Estimation

Estimate. Circle greater than 50 or less than 50.
Use tens and ones blocks to check.

13 Sam has 54 trading cards. He gives away 13 of the cards. How many cards does he have left?

more than 50 less than 50

14 Suppose Sam does not give away any cards. Instead, he buys 18 more. How many cards does he have?

more than 50 less than 50

HOME ACTIVITY • Have your child use his or her popcorn bags and pieces (explained on page 200) to show you how he or she solved some of the problems on this page.

Name ______________________________

Review/Test
Chapter 14

CHECK ■ Concepts and Skills

Subtract.

1 $5 - 1 =$ ______

5 tens − 1 ten = ______ tens

$50 - 10 =$ ______

2 $9 - 3 =$ ______

9 tens − 3 tens = ______ tens

$90 - 30 =$ ______

Choose a method to solve the problems.

3
$$\begin{array}{r} 45 \\ -10 \\ \hline \end{array}$$

4
$$\begin{array}{r} 89 \\ -\ \ 3 \\ \hline \end{array}$$

Use Workmat 3 and tens and ones blocks. Find the difference.

5

tens	ones
☐	☐
4	2
− 1	6

6

tens	ones
☐	☐
2	3
− 1	9

Use Workmat 3 and tens and ones blocks.

Subtract.	Do you need to regroup?	Subtract. Write how many are left.
7 $21 - 6 =$ ______	Yes No	______ tens ______ ones
8 $49 - 7 =$ ______	Yes No	______ tens ______ ones
9 $53 - 47 =$ ______	Yes No	______
10 $72 - 32 =$ ______	Yes No	______

Name ______________________________

Standardized Test Prep
Chapters 1–14

Choose the best answer for questions 1–7.

1

$$\begin{array}{r} 80 \\ -\ 50 \\ \hline \end{array}$$

30 ○ 40 ○ 120 ○ 130 ○

2

$$\begin{array}{r} 73 \\ -\ \ 2 \\ \hline \end{array}$$

61 ○ 63 ○ 70 ○ 71 ○

3

$$\begin{array}{r} 57 \\ -\ 28 \\ \hline \end{array}$$

29 ○ 31 ○ 55 ○ 85 ○

4

$$\begin{array}{r} 44 \\ -\ 37 \\ \hline \end{array}$$

1 ○ 7 ○ 3 ○ 81 ○

5

$$\begin{array}{r} 93 \\ -\ 20 \\ \hline \end{array}$$

23 ○ 53 ○ 63 ○ 73 ○

6

$$\begin{array}{r} 63 \\ -\ \ 5 \\ \hline \end{array}$$

56 ○ 57 ○ 58 ○ 62 ○

7 Amanda has 5 pink erasers and 13 blue erasers in her pencil box. How many erasers are there in her pencil box?

5 ○ 8 ○ 17 ○ 18 ○

Show What You Know

8 Complete each problem. Choose numbers that will **not** need to be regrouped.

_____ − 6 = _____ _____ − 7 = _____

_____ − 8 = _____ _____ − 9 = _____

CHAPTER 15 2-Digit Subtraction

What subtraction problems do you see at the construction site?

School Home Connection

Dear Family,

Today we started Chapter 15. We will look at more ways to subtract 2-digit numbers. Here is the math vocabulary and an activity for us to do together at home.

Love,

____

My Math Words

estimate differences
rounding

Vocabulary

estimate differences Find *about* how many are left by rounding each number to the closer ten and then subtracting the tens.

Estimate 87 – 32 as 90 – 30.

90 – 30 = 60

So 87 – 32 is about 60.

rounding A way to estimate an answer. In this chapter, we round to the closer ten.

Activity

Cut paper into squares. On each square, write a number from 1-50. Have your child choose 2 squares and subtract the smaller number from the number on the other square. Continue until all the squares have been used.

Books to Share

To read about subtraction with your child, look for these books in your local library.

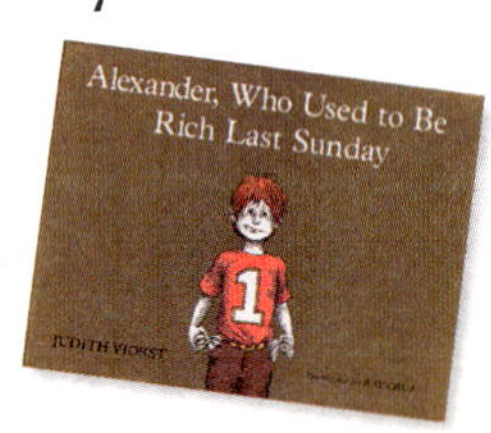

Alexander, Who Used to be Rich Last Sunday,
by Judith Viorst,
Simon & Schuster, 1988.

Caps for Sale,
by Esphyr Slobodkina,
HarperCollins, 1999.

Visit *The Learning Site* for additional ideas and activities. www.harcourtschool.com

Name ______________________________

Subtract 2-Digit Numbers

42 − 15 = _____

Step 1

Show 42.
Look at the ones.
Are there enough ones to subtract 5?

Yes   (No)

tens	ones
☐	☐
4	2
− 1	5

Step 2

Regroup 1 ten as 10 ones.
Now there are 12 ones.
Subtract 5 from 12.
Write how many ones are left.

tens	ones
3	12
~~4~~	~~2~~
− 1	5
	7

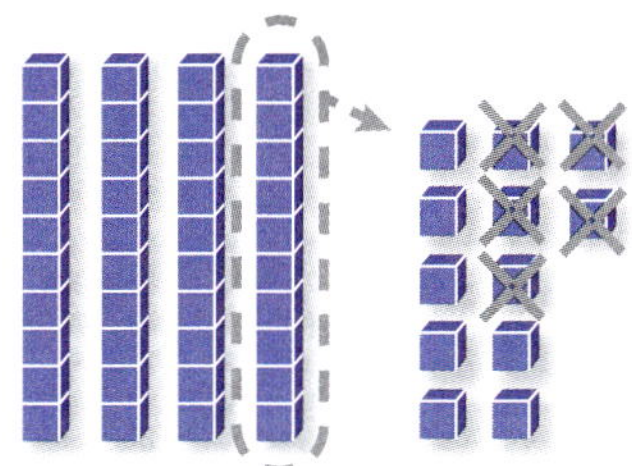

Step 3

Subtract the tens.
Write how many tens are left.

tens	ones
3	12
~~4~~	~~2~~
− 1	5
2	7

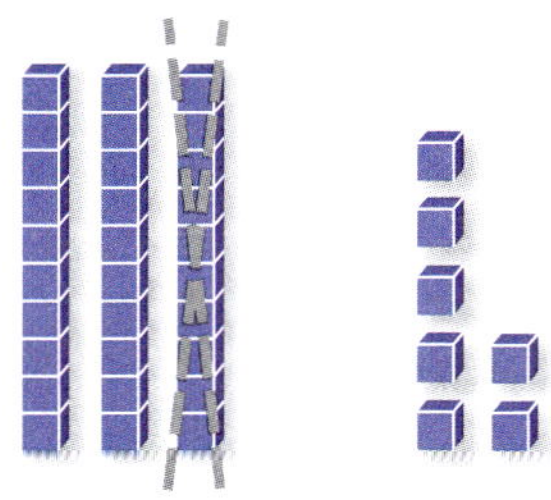

Use Workmat 3 and .
Subtract. Regroup if you need to.

1.

tens	ones
☐	☐
3	8
− 1	8

2.

tens	ones
☐	☐
4	0
− 2	7

3.

tens	ones
☐	☐
2	7
−	9

4.

tens	ones
☐	☐
5	1
− 3	6

Talk About It ■ Reasoning

How do you know when you need to regroup?

Practice

Circle the problems in which you need to regroup.
Subtract. Regroup if you need to.

1

tens	ones
6	15
~~7~~	~~5~~
− 2	9
4	6

2

tens	ones
☐	☐
8	3
− 2	7

3

tens	ones
☐	☐
6	5
−	5

4

tens	ones
☐	☐
7	1
− 1	9

5

tens	ones
☐	☐
9	1
− 1	6

6

tens	ones
☐	☐
8	0
− 4	2

7

tens	ones
☐	☐
5	7
− 2	8

8

tens	ones
☐	☐
6	2
− 3	2

9

tens	ones
☐	☐
9	5
− 4	8

10

tens	ones
☐	☐
3	7
− 1	9

11

tens	ones
☐	☐
8	9
− 4	8

12

tens	ones
☐	☐
6	3
−	7

Mixed Review

Write >, <, or = in the circle.

13 26 ◯ 36 | **14** 50 ◯ 49 | **15** 35 ◯ 32

16 94 ◯ 49 | **17** 23 ◯ 23 | **18** 24 ◯ 42

HOME ACTIVITY • Ask your child to tell you how he or she knows when to regroup when subtracting.

Name ______________________________

Rewrite 2-Digit Subtraction

How would you write 62 − 39 to solve?
Rewrite the problem to subtract.

tens	ones
5	12
~~6~~	~~2~~
−3	9
2	3

Write the larger number on top. Write the smaller number under it with the tens under the tens and the ones under the ones.

Rewrite the numbers in each problem.
Then subtract.

1. 54 − 27

tens	ones
4	14
~~5~~	~~4~~
−2	7
2	7

2. 45 − 38

tens	ones
−	

3. 76 − 46

tens	ones
−	

4. 62 − 8

tens	ones
−	

5. 33 − 15

tens	ones
−	

6. 94 − 65

tens	ones
−	

7. 43 − 19

tens	ones
−	

8. 46 − 28

tens	ones
−	

Talk About It ■ Reasoning

Why do you need to write the larger number on top when you want to subtract?

Practice

Rewrite the numbers in each problem.
Then subtract.

1. 51 − 17

tens	ones
4	11
~~5~~	~~1~~
− 1	7
3	4

2. 29 − 23

tens	ones
−	

3. 42 − 9

tens	ones
−	

4. 97 − 48

tens	ones
−	

5. 56 − 45

tens	ones
−	

6. 38 − 14

tens	ones
−	

7. 66 − 7

tens	ones
−	

8. 80 − 18

tens	ones
−	

9. 93 − 37

tens	ones
−	

10. 45 − 38

tens	ones
−	

11. 74 − 27

tens	ones
−	

12. 22 − 12

tens	ones
−	

Problem Solving ■ Estimating

Estimate. Circle the reasonable answer.

13. Juan has 82 football cards and 65 baseball cards. About how many more football cards does he have?

more than 20

less than 20

HOME ACTIVITY • Name a 2-digit subtraction problem starting with any number up to 99. Have your child write the problem and then subtract to solve. Repeat several times.

Name ______________________

More 2-Digit Subtraction

Alexander had 31 building blocks. He used 12 to build a tower. How many blocks does he have left?

Step 1
Are there enough ones to subtract 2?

$$\begin{array}{r} 31 \\ -\,12 \\ \hline \end{array}$$

Step 2
Regroup if you need to.
Subtract the ones.

$$\begin{array}{r} {\scriptstyle 2\,11} \\ \not{3}\not{1} \\ -\,12 \\ \hline 9 \end{array}$$

Step 3
Subtract the tens.
Write how many.

$$\begin{array}{r} {\scriptstyle 2\,11} \\ \not{3}\not{1} \\ -\,12 \\ \hline 19 \end{array}$$

Alexander has __19__ blocks left.

Circle the problems in which you need to regroup. Then subtract.

1. $\begin{array}{r} {\scriptstyle 6\,15} \\ \not{7}\not{5} \\ -\,47 \\ \hline 28 \end{array}$
2. $\begin{array}{r} 60 \\ -\,2 \\ \hline \end{array}$
3. $\begin{array}{r} 58 \\ -\,39 \\ \hline \end{array}$
4. $\begin{array}{r} 46 \\ -\,23 \\ \hline \end{array}$
5. $\begin{array}{r} 96 \\ -\,27 \\ \hline \end{array}$
6. $\begin{array}{r} 92 \\ -\,57 \\ \hline \end{array}$
7. $\begin{array}{r} 59 \\ -\,25 \\ \hline \end{array}$
8. $\begin{array}{r} 40 \\ -\,21 \\ \hline \end{array}$
9. $\begin{array}{r} 33 \\ -\,8 \\ \hline \end{array}$
10. $\begin{array}{r} 80 \\ -\,46 \\ \hline \end{array}$

Talk About It ■ Reasoning

What did Dan do wrong when he solved this problem?

Practice

Circle the problems in which you need to regroup.
Then subtract.

1. $\begin{array}{r} \overset{8}{\cancel{9}}\overset{14}{\cancel{4}} \\ -55 \\ \hline 39 \end{array}$	2. $\begin{array}{r} 36 \\ -29 \\ \hline \end{array}$	3. $\begin{array}{r} 76 \\ -46 \\ \hline \end{array}$	4. $\begin{array}{r} 81 \\ -27 \\ \hline \end{array}$	
5. $\begin{array}{r} 52 \\ -37 \\ \hline \end{array}$	6. $\begin{array}{r} 92 \\ -11 \\ \hline \end{array}$	7. $\begin{array}{r} 40 \\ -37 \\ \hline \end{array}$	8. $\begin{array}{r} 25 \\ -6 \\ \hline \end{array}$	9. $\begin{array}{r} 38 \\ -19 \\ \hline \end{array}$
10. $\begin{array}{r} 92 \\ -63 \\ \hline \end{array}$	11. $\begin{array}{r} 64 \\ -29 \\ \hline \end{array}$	12. $\begin{array}{r} 73 \\ -55 \\ \hline \end{array}$	13. $\begin{array}{r} 43 \\ -26 \\ \hline \end{array}$	14. $\begin{array}{r} 36 \\ -14 \\ \hline \end{array}$
15. $\begin{array}{r} 73 \\ -4 \\ \hline \end{array}$	16. $\begin{array}{r} 95 \\ -52 \\ \hline \end{array}$	17. $\begin{array}{r} 90 \\ -26 \\ \hline \end{array}$	18. $\begin{array}{r} 41 \\ -17 \\ \hline \end{array}$	19. $\begin{array}{r} 54 \\ -36 \\ \hline \end{array}$

Problem Solving ▪ Number Sense

20. Write the missing numbers. How many times can you subtract 13 from 65? ______

$\begin{array}{r} 65 \\ -13 \\ \hline 52 \end{array}$ → $\begin{array}{r} 52 \\ -13 \\ \hline \square \end{array}$ → $\begin{array}{r} \square \\ -13 \\ \hline \square \end{array}$ → $\begin{array}{r} \square \\ -13 \\ \hline \square \end{array}$ → $\begin{array}{r} \square \\ -13 \\ \hline \square \end{array}$

HOME ACTIVITY • Have your child choose a problem on this page and tell you the steps he or she followed to subtract.

Name ______________________________

UNDERSTAND PLAN SOLVE CHECK

Problem Solving
Estimate Differences

Tosha has 22 peanuts. She eats 14 peanuts. How many peanuts does Tosha have left? Estimate. Then solve.

UNDERSTAND

You need to find out how many peanuts Tosha has left. You want to estimate and then solve the problem.

PLAN

Use a number line to round.

SOLVE

10 11 12 13 (14) 15 16 17 18 19 **20** 21 (22) 23 24 25 26 27 28 29 **30**

Is 22 closer to 20 or 30? 20

Is 14 closer to 10 or 20? 10

Tosha has about 10 peanuts left.

estimate
20 − 10 10

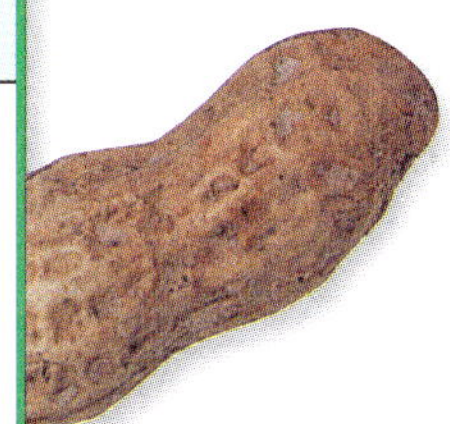

Now solve. Subtract to find how many peanuts Tosha has left.

solve
1 12 22 − 14 8

8 is close to 10, so the answer makes sense.

CHECK

How does your estimate help you know if your answer makes sense?

Practice

Estimate by rounding. Then solve.

40 41 42 43 44 45 46 47 48 49 **50** 51 52 53 54 55 56 57 58 59 **60**

1. Tim has 59 tiny toy cars. He gives 43 cars away. How many toy cars does he have left?

   16 cars

2. There are 48 red beads and 42 blue beads in the set. How many more red beads than blue beads are there?

   _______ more red beads

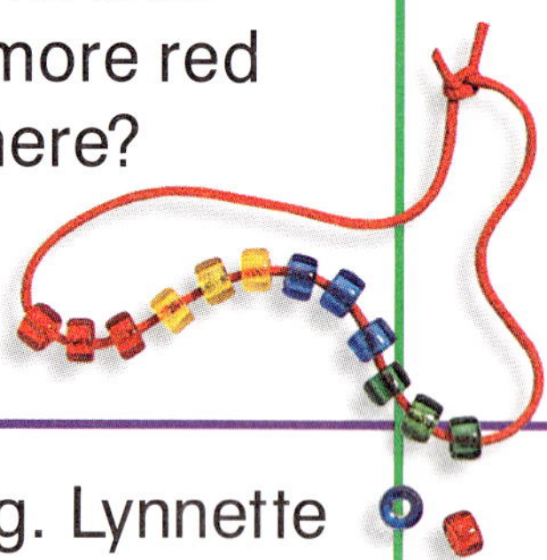

3. There are 59 marbles in a bag. Lynnette takes out 52 marbles to play. How many marbles are left in the bag?

   _______ marbles

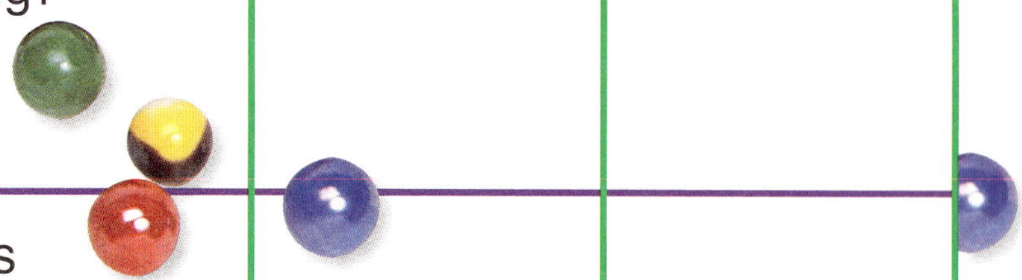

4. Virginia has 58 blocks. Lisa has 41 blocks. How many more blocks does Virginia have?

   _______ more blocks

	estimate	solve
1	$60 - 40 = 20$	$59 - 43 = 16$
2		
3		
4		

Math Journal

Write About It

Write a story in which someone estimates some numbers. Use numbers that are 99 or less.

HOME ACTIVITY • Have your child practice estimating differences while you are at the supermarket. Pick two items with prices up to 99¢. Ask your child to round the numbers to estimate the difference.

Name ____________________

Use Addition to Check Subtraction

Algebra

Subtract. To check your answer, add back the number you subtracted. The sum should be the number you subtracted from.

Subtract.		**Add to check.**	
$\begin{array}{r} \overset{5\,13}{\cancel{6}\cancel{3}} \\ -38 \\ \hline 25 \end{array}$	Add these numbers to check.	$\begin{array}{r} \overset{1}{25} \\ +38 \\ \hline 63 \end{array}$	Is this the number you subtracted from? If so, your subtraction is correct.

Subtract. Add to check.

1. $\begin{array}{r} \overset{3\,11}{\cancel{4}\cancel{1}} \\ -15 \\ \hline 26 \end{array}$ $\quad$ $\begin{array}{r} \overset{1}{26} \\ +15 \\ \hline 41 \end{array}$

2. $\begin{array}{r} 74 \\ -46 \\ \hline \end{array}$

3. $\begin{array}{r} 40 \\ -19 \\ \hline \end{array}$

4. $\begin{array}{r} 67 \\ -35 \\ \hline \end{array}$

5. $\begin{array}{r} 83 \\ -58 \\ \hline \end{array}$

6. $\begin{array}{r} 56 \\ -28 \\ \hline \end{array}$

Talk About It ■ **Reasoning**

How can you use addition to check the answer for a subtraction problem? Explain why it works.

Practice

Subtract.
Add to check.

1. $\begin{array}{r} \overset{2}{\cancel{3}}\overset{13}{\cancel{3}} \\ -17 \\ \hline 16 \end{array}$ $\begin{array}{r} 16 \\ +17 \\ \hline 33 \end{array}$

2. $\begin{array}{r} 70 \\ -43 \\ \hline \end{array}$

3. $\begin{array}{r} 94 \\ -56 \\ \hline \end{array}$

4. $\begin{array}{r} 30 \\ -17 \\ \hline \end{array}$

5. $\begin{array}{r} 48 \\ -25 \\ \hline \end{array}$

6. $\begin{array}{r} 83 \\ -34 \\ \hline \end{array}$

7. $\begin{array}{r} 36 \\ -14 \\ \hline \end{array}$

8. $\begin{array}{r} 53 \\ -26 \\ \hline \end{array}$

9. $\begin{array}{r} 75 \\ -37 \\ \hline \end{array}$

Algebra

Write and solve three problems, using only the numbers shown.

10. $\begin{array}{r} 63 \\ -39 \\ \hline 24 \end{array}$ $\begin{array}{r} \square \\ -\ \square \\ \hline \square \end{array}$ $\begin{array}{r} \square \\ +\ \square \\ \hline \square \end{array}$ $\begin{array}{r} \square \\ +\ \square \\ \hline \square \end{array}$

HOME ACTIVITY • Have your child show you how he or she checks subtraction answers by adding.

Name ______________________________

Review/Test
Chapter 15

CHECK ■ Concepts and Skills

Use Workmat 3 and ▭ ▫.
Subtract. Regroup if you need to.

1.

tens	ones
☐	☐
6	5
− 3	8

2.

tens	ones
☐	☐
8	8
− 5	3

Rewrite the numbers.
Then subtract.

3. 43 − 28 = ______

tens	ones
−	

Subtract.

4.
$$\begin{array}{r} 60 \\ -25 \\ \hline \end{array}$$

5.
$$\begin{array}{r} 74 \\ -45 \\ \hline \end{array}$$

Subtract. Add to check.

6.
$$\begin{array}{r} 94 \\ -67 \\ \hline \end{array}$$

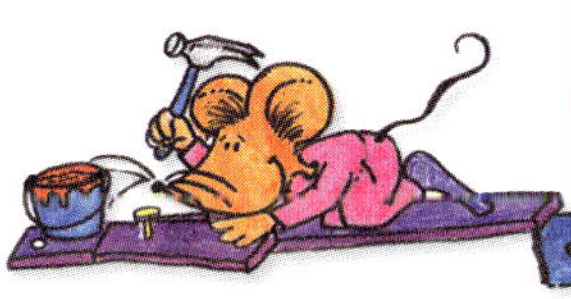

CHECK ■ Problem Solving

Estimate by rounding. Then solve.

40 41 42 43 44 45 46 47 48 49 **50** 51 52 53 54 55 56 57 58 59 **60**

7. There are 58 toy cars in a bin.
Carl takes out 49 to play with.
How many toy cars are left
in the bin?

______ toy cars

estimate	solve

Name ______________________________

Standardized Test Prep
Chapters 1–15

Choose the best answer for questions 1–5.

1

$$\begin{array}{r} 63 \\ -\,47 \\ \hline \end{array}$$

16 ○ 17 ○ 27 ○ 110 ○

2

$$\begin{array}{r} 80 \\ -\,79 \\ \hline \end{array}$$

1 ○ 10 ○ 19 ○ 159 ○

3 Which is another way to write 47 − 9 = ______?

$\begin{array}{r} 74 \\ -\,19 \\ \hline \end{array}$ ○ $\begin{array}{r} 47 \\ -\,9 \\ \hline \end{array}$ ○ $\begin{array}{r} 74 \\ -\,9 \\ \hline \end{array}$ ○ $\begin{array}{r} 47 \\ -\,19 \\ \hline \end{array}$ ○

4 Which number is even?

1 ○ 17 ○ 26 ○ 35 ○

5 There are 38 pencils in a cup. During a math lesson, the class uses 21 pencils from the cup. Which is the best estimate of how many pencils are left in the cup?

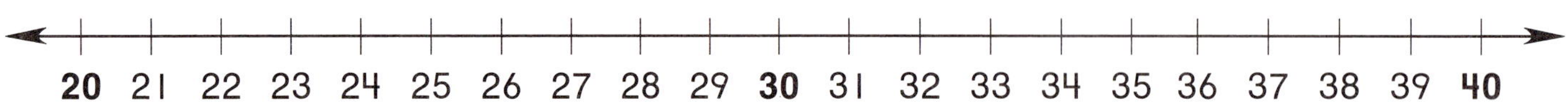

about 10 ○ about 20 ○ about 40 ○ about 70 ○

Show What You Know

6 Write a subtraction problem.
Use numbers that have tens and ones.
Write an addition problem to check it.

$\begin{array}{r} \square \\ -\,\square \\ \hline \end{array}$ $\begin{array}{r} \square \\ +\,\square \\ \hline \end{array}$ | $\begin{array}{r} \square \\ -\,\square \\ \hline \end{array}$ $\begin{array}{r} \square \\ +\,\square \\ \hline \end{array}$

CHAPTER 16

Practice 2-Digit Subtraction

What subtraction stories can you write about this picture?

School Home Connection

Dear Family,

Today we started Chapter 16. We will subtract 2-digit numbers, use mental math, and add and subtract amounts of money. Here is the math vocabulary and an activity for us to do together at home.

Love,

____

My Math Words

mental math

Vocabulary

mental math A way to subtract in your head without using pencil or paper.

$$\begin{array}{r} 36 \\ -17 \\ \hline ? \end{array}$$

Add more to make the smaller number a ten.

$$17 + 3 = 20$$

Add the same number to the larger number.

$$36 + 3 = 39$$

Subtract your answers.

$$\begin{array}{r} 39 \\ -20 \\ \hline 19 \end{array}$$

So,

$$\begin{array}{r} 36 \\ -17 \\ \hline 19 \end{array}$$

Visit *The Learning Site* for additional ideas and activities. www.harcourtschool.com

Activity

Look at grocery store ads for items that cost 99¢ or less. Have your child use these numbers to write subtraction problems and find the differences.

Books to Share

To read about subtraction with your child, look for these books in your local library.

Anno's Math Games II,
by Mitsumaso Anno,
Putnam & Grosset Group, 1989.

Country Fair,
by Elisha Cooper,
HarperCollins, 1997.

Monster Money Book,
by Loreen Leedy,
Holiday House, 2000.

Name ______________________________

Use Mental Math to Find Differences

$$\begin{array}{r} 27 \\ -\ 18 \\ \hline ? \end{array}$$

Step 1	Step 2	Step 3
Add more to make the smaller number a ten.	Add the same number to the larger number.	Subtract your answers.
$\begin{array}{r} 27 \\ -\ 18 \\ \hline \end{array}$	$27 + 2 = 29$ $18 + 2 = 20$	$\begin{array}{r} 29 \\ -\ 20 \\ \hline 9 \end{array}$
$18 + 2 = 20$		So, $\begin{array}{r} 27 \\ -\ 18 \\ \hline 9 \end{array}$

You can use mental math to subtract in your head.

Use what you learned to find the difference.

	Add the same number to both numbers.	Subtract.	
1 $\begin{array}{r} 35 \\ -\ 19 \\ \hline ? \end{array}$ Add more to make 19 a ten.	$35 + \underline{1} = \underline{36}$ $19 + \underline{1} = \underline{20}$	$\begin{array}{r} 36 \\ -\ 20 \\ \hline 16 \end{array}$	So, $\begin{array}{r} 35 \\ -\ 19 \\ \hline 16 \end{array}$
2 $\begin{array}{r} 76 \\ -\ 38 \\ \hline ? \end{array}$	$76 + \underline{\quad} = \underline{\quad}$ $38 + \underline{\quad} = \underline{\quad}$	$\begin{array}{r} \square \\ -\ \square \\ \hline \square \end{array}$	So, $\begin{array}{r} 76 \\ -\ 38 \\ \hline \square \end{array}$

Talk About It ■ **Reasoning**

Why is it easier to subtract 20 from 29 than 18 from 27?

Practice

Use what you learned to find the difference.

	Add the same number to both numbers.	Subtract.	
1 $\begin{array}{r} 65 \\ -\ 28 \\ \hline ? \end{array}$ Add more to make 28 a ten.	$65 + \underline{\ 2\ } = \underline{\ 67\ }$ $28 + \underline{\ 2\ } = \underline{\ 30\ }$	$\begin{array}{r} 67 \\ -\ 30 \\ \hline 37 \end{array}$	So, $\begin{array}{r} 65 \\ -\ 28 \\ \hline 37 \end{array}$
2 $\begin{array}{r} 46 \\ -\ 19 \\ \hline ? \end{array}$	$46 + \underline{\quad} = \underline{\quad}$ $19 + \underline{\quad} = \underline{\quad}$	$\begin{array}{r} \square \\ -\ \square \\ \hline \square \end{array}$	So, $\begin{array}{r} 46 \\ -\ 19 \\ \hline \end{array}$

Try subtracting these numbers in your head.

3 $\begin{array}{r} 71 \\ -\ 57 \\ \hline \end{array}$

4 $\begin{array}{r} 64 \\ -\ 49 \\ \hline \end{array}$

5 $\begin{array}{r} 35 \\ -\ 26 \\ \hline \end{array}$

6 $\begin{array}{r} 83 \\ -\ 56 \\ \hline \end{array}$

Mixed Review

Write the time. Draw the minute hand to show the time.

7 25 minutes after 3

___:___

8 10 minutes after 1

___:___

9 45 minutes after 6

___:___

HOME ACTIVITY • Have your child tell how he or she subtracted the numbers in the exercises on this page.

Name ______________________________

Practice Subtracting 2-Digit Numbers

There are many different ways to subtract.
You can subtract in your head or you can use paper and pencil.

Count back by tens.
49 − 30 = 19
Say 49. Count back 3 tens.
39, 29, 19

Count back by ones.
37 − 3 = 34
Say 37.
Count back 3 ones.
36, 35, 34

Regroup.

$$\begin{array}{r} {\scriptstyle 4\ \ 15} \\ \not{5}\not{5}¢ \\ -\ 36¢ \\ \hline 19¢ \end{array}$$

Regroup 1 ten as 10 ones.
Subtract 6 from 15.
Write how many ones are left.

Subtract the tens.
Write how many tens are left.

Subtract. Choose a strategy.

1

67	34¢	51	96	85¢	50
− 2	− 15¢	− 43	− 10	− 26¢	− 40
65					

2

19	51	75¢	60	58	87
− 5	− 26	− 17¢	− 20	− 58	− 39

3

54¢	90	68	42	95¢	72
− 25¢	− 50	− 31	− 37	− 59¢	− 46

Talk About It ▪ **Reasoning**
Which problems did you subtract in your head? Why?

Practice

Subtract. Then use the code to read the message.

1 – A	6 – F	11 – K	15 – O	19 – S	23 – W
2 – B	7 – G	12 – L	16 – P	20 – T	24 – X
3 – C	8 – H	13 – M	17 – Q	21 – U	25 – Y
4 – D	9 – I	14 – N	18 – R	22 – V	26 – Z
5 – E	10 – J				

Why did the sailor go shopping?

41 − 39	53 − 48	29 − 26	12 − 11	32 − 11	39 − 20	24 − 19
2	___	___	___	___	___	___
B	___	___	___	___	___	___

72 − 53	31 − 23	39 − 34	24 − 12	46 − 37	16 − 5	36 − 31	16 − 12
___	___	___	___	___	___	___	___
___	___	___	___	___	___	___	___

54 − 34	16 − 8	20 − 15	47 − 28	50 − 49	20 − 8	42 − 37	56 − 37
___	___	___	___	___	___	___	___
___	___	___	___	___	___	___	___

HOME ACTIVITY • You and your child can have fun using the code to write "secret" notes to each other.

Name ______________________________

Add and Subtract Money

Mrs. Scott buys juice for 67¢ and nuts for 24¢. How much money does she spend in all?

1
67¢
+ 24¢
91¢

Mrs. Scott spends 91¢.

Mike has 50¢. He spends 35¢ on a boat. How much money does he have left?

4 10
50¢
− 35¢
15¢

Mike has 15¢ left.

Circle the + or − . Then solve.

1

56¢	75¢	90¢	44¢	65¢	29¢
+ 9¢	− 18¢	− 87¢	+ 28¢	− 25¢	+ 24¢

2

50¢	88¢	23¢	7¢	48¢	96¢
− 35¢	− 49¢	+ 53¢	+ 64¢	+ 14¢	− 52¢

3

27¢	76¢	63¢	34¢	86¢	49¢
− 19¢	+ 20¢	− 37¢	+ 59¢	− 55¢	+ 39¢

Talk About It ■ **Reasoning**

How is adding amounts of money the same as adding 2-digit numbers? How is it different?

Practice

Circle the + or −.
Then solve.

1 69¢ −33¢ 36¢	54¢ +18¢	92¢ − 9¢	27¢ +40¢	81¢ −26¢	39¢ −25¢
2 43¢ −25¢	92¢ −86¢	35¢ +25¢	8¢ +64¢	76¢ −25¢	87¢ −15¢
3 73¢ + 7¢	84¢ +11¢	46¢ −38¢	7¢ +30¢	78¢ −64¢	76¢ −72¢
4 71¢ −32¢	9¢ +41¢	33¢ − 9¢	18¢ +64¢	41¢ −13¢	61¢ +27¢

Problem Solving ■ Application

Solve.

5 One store sells a toy plane for 94¢. Another store sells the same plane for 76¢. How much more is the plane at the first store than at the second?

______ more

HOME ACTIVITY • Have your child look in supermarket flyers and add or subtract prices for two items that together cost less than 99¢.

Name ____________________

UNDERSTAND › PLAN › SOLVE › CHECK

Problem Solving
Choose the Operation

Add or subtract. Write the sum or difference.

1 How much money would you need to buy a bear and a yo-yo?

$$\begin{array}{r} 67¢ \\ + \; 18¢ \\ \hline 85¢ \end{array}$$

You would need 85¢.

2 You have 55¢. You buy a puppet. How much money do you have left?

You have ___ ¢

○ ___ ¢

___ ¢

3 How much money would you need to buy a boat and a jump rope?

___ ¢

○ ___ ¢

___ ¢

4 How much money would you need to buy a train car and a ball?

___ ¢

○ ___ ¢

___ ¢

5 You want to buy a bear. You have 15¢. How much more money do you need?

Bear costs ___ ¢

You have ○ ___ ¢

You need ___ ¢

Practice

Add or subtract. Write the sum or difference.

1 How much money would you need to buy a puppet and a car?

30¢
\+ 59¢
89¢

2 You want to buy a train engine. You have 20¢. How much more money do you need?

___ ¢
○ ___ ¢
___ ¢

3 You have 90¢. You buy a car. How much money do you have left?

You have ___ ¢
○ ___ ¢
___ ¢

4 How much money would you need to buy a bear and a ball?

___ ¢
○ ___ ¢
___ ¢

5 You want to buy a bear. You have 50¢. How much more money do you need?

___ ¢
○ ___ ¢
___ ¢

6 How much money would you need to buy 2 puppets?

___ ¢
○ ___ ¢
___ ¢

Math Journal

Write About It

Write a math story about toys on two shelves. Use numbers up to 50. The story can use addition or subtraction.

HOME ACTIVITY • Have your child model with coins adding the prices of two grocery items that together cost less than 99¢. He or she can also subtract the price of an item from 99¢.

Name ______________________

Review/Test
Chapter 16

CHECK ■ Concepts and Skills

Find the difference.

	Add the same number to both numbers.	Subtract.	
1 52 − 18 = ?	52 + ____ = ____ 18 + ____ = ____	☐ − ☐ ☐	So, 52 − 18 = ☐

Subtract. Choose a strategy.

2 $67 - 39$

3 $70 - 40$

4 $39 - 21$

5 $41 - 8$

Circle the + or −. Then solve.

6 33¢ + 27¢

7 82¢ − 45¢

8 87¢ − 8¢

9 52¢ + 44¢

CHECK ■ Problem Solving

Add or subtract. Write the sum or difference.

10 You have 75¢. You buy a yo-yo. How much money do you have left?

You have ☐ ¢

○ ☐ ¢

☐ ¢

11 How much money would you need to buy a train car and a rope?

☐ ¢

○ ☐ ¢

☐ ¢

Name ______________________________

Standardized Test Prep
Chapters 1–16

Choose the best answer for questions 1–6.

1

$$\begin{array}{r} 34 \\ -\ 19 \\ \hline \end{array}$$

15 ○ 16 ○ 49 ○ 53 ○

2

$$\begin{array}{r} 75 \\ -\ \ 8 \\ \hline \end{array}$$

67 ○ 73 ○ 77 ○ 83 ○

3

$$\begin{array}{r} 97¢ \\ -\ 49¢ \\ \hline \end{array}$$

38¢ ○ 42¢ ○ 47¢ ○ 48¢ ○

4

$$\begin{array}{r} 9¢ \\ +\ 10¢ \\ \hline \end{array}$$

19¢ ○ 20¢ ○ 29¢ ○ 39¢ ○

5 Sarah wants to buy a baseball. She has 85¢. The baseball costs 99¢. Which tells how much more money Sarah will need to buy the baseball?

85¢ − 99¢ ○ 99¢ − 85¢ ○ 58¢ + 99¢ ○ 99¢ − 58¢ ○

6 How much money is shown?

55¢ ○ 56¢ ○ 66¢ ○ 65¢ ○

Show What You Know

7 Use these numbers. Write them in the boxes to make each difference.

44	15	12	59

$$\begin{array}{r} \square \\ -\ \square \\ \hline 47 \end{array} \qquad \begin{array}{r} \square \\ -\ \square \\ \hline 29 \end{array}$$

The Picnic Lunch

written by Jo Sumara
illustrated by Ken Laidlaw

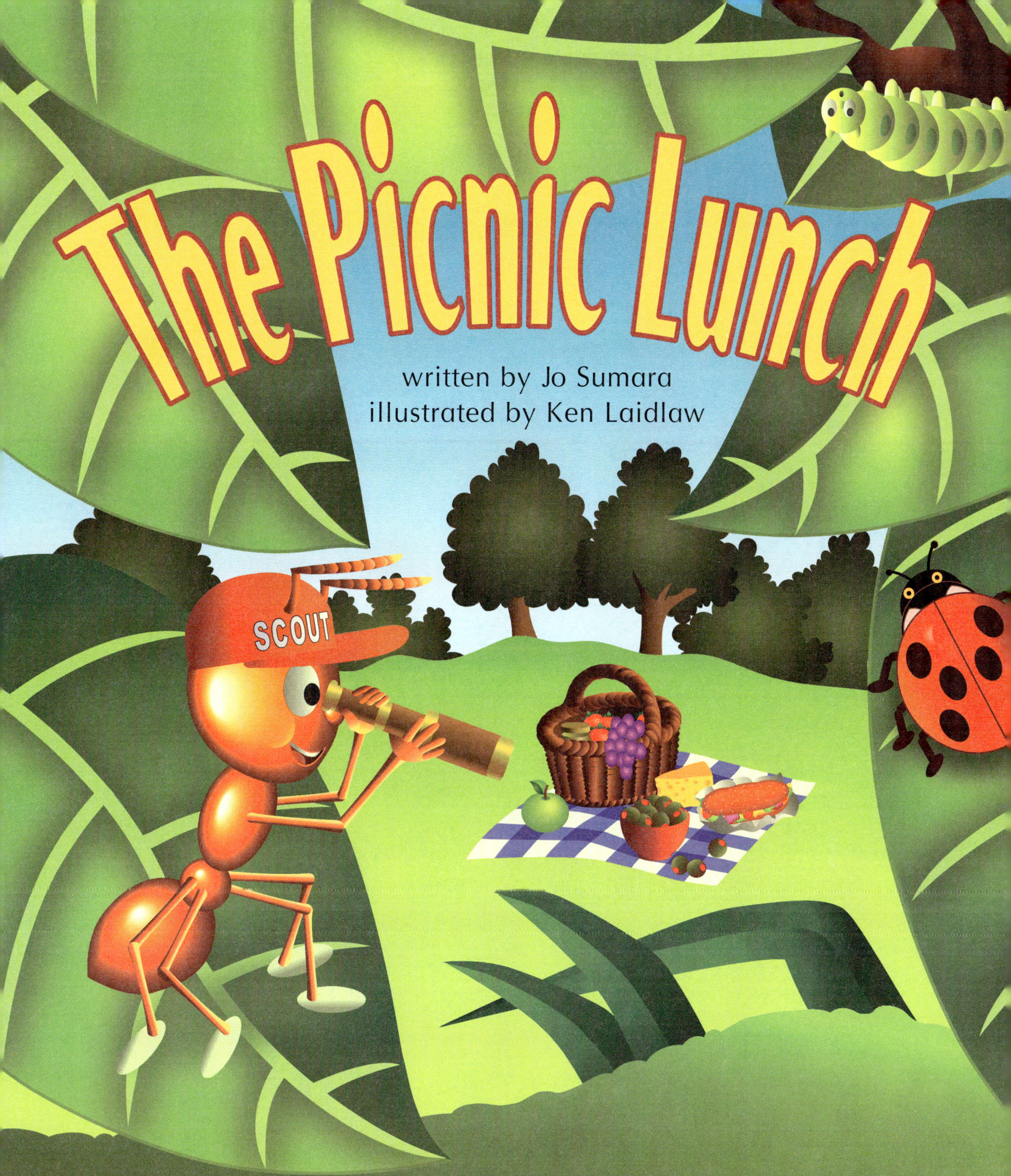

This book will help me review 2-digit addition and subtraction.

This book belongs to ____________________.

A

Andy Ant could not believe his eyes.

Was it really a picnic?
It looked like a picnic.
It smelled like a picnic.
It was a picnic!

What luck! This was Andy's first day as a scout. He wanted everyone to be proud of him.

Andy yelled, “I found a picnic!”

“Yippee! Hooray!” the other ants shouted.

No one had found a picnic in a long time. All the ants danced and cheered for Andy. He felt very proud.

After Andy told the queen, she gave orders to the ants. The ants prepared for the picnic. 40 ants and then 30 more lined up.

"Which way is the picnic?" asked the ants. Andy pointed, and the ants marched away.

How many ants were sent to the picnic? ______

When the ants got to the picnic, they were amazed. There were so many foods to choose from. It took 5 ants to carry an olive. It took 20 of them to lift the cheese. They started the long, hard walk back home.

How many ants took the olive and cheese home? ______

The queen sent 68 strong ants to get the sandwich. It turned out that 47 could pick it up. What did the other ants do?

They carried Andy!

How many ants carried Andy? ______

At home, all the ants greeted Andy. They were so proud of him.

"Hooray for Andy!" they cheered.

The queen invited her best scout to sit at her table for the BIG picnic.

Name ____________________

A Stroll Through the Garden

Use your problem solving skills to write the missing sign. Draw a line to show the way out of the maze.

Stretch Your Thinking ■ Draw a maze of your own for your classmates to solve.

Name ______________________________

Challenge
2-Digit Addition

1	2	3

$$\begin{array}{r} 1 \\ +\ 2 \\ \hline 3 \end{array} \qquad \begin{array}{r} 2 \\ +\ 3 \\ \hline 5 \end{array} \qquad \begin{array}{r} 1 \\ +\ 3 \\ \hline 4 \end{array}$$

Use each number one time in each problem.
Try to make the greatest possible sum.

1	2	3	4

$$\begin{array}{r} \square\square \\ +\ \square\square \\ \hline \end{array} \qquad \begin{array}{r} \square\square \\ +\ \square\square \\ \hline \end{array} \qquad \begin{array}{r} \square\square \\ +\ \square\square \\ \hline \end{array} \qquad \begin{array}{r} \square\square \\ +\ \square\square \\ \hline \end{array}$$

$$\begin{array}{r} \square\square \\ +\ \square\square \\ \hline \end{array} \qquad \begin{array}{r} \square\square \\ +\ \square\square \\ \hline \end{array} \qquad \begin{array}{r} \square\square \\ +\ \square\square \\ \hline \end{array} \qquad \begin{array}{r} \square\square \\ +\ \square\square \\ \hline \end{array}$$

What is the greatest sum that you found? ________

Name ______________________________

Skills and Concepts

Use Workmat 3 and tens and ones blocks. Add.

Show.	Join the ones. Can you make a ten? If so, regroup 10 ones as 1 ten.	Write how many in all.
1 56 + 4 = _____	Yes No	_____ tens _____ ones
2 17 + 16 = _____	Yes No	_____ tens _____ ones

Add.

3
$$\begin{array}{r} 62 \\ +\ 3 \\ \hline \end{array}$$

4
$$\begin{array}{r} 62 \\ +\ 30 \\ \hline \end{array}$$

5

tens	ones
□	
3	7
+2	9

6

tens	ones
□	
7	3
+1	7

7 Rewrite. Then add.

64 + 7

tens	ones
□	
+	

8 Use mental math to add 28 + 65.

_____ + _____ = _____

_____ + _____ = _____

_____ + _____ = _____

Use Workmat 3 and [tens blocks] [ones blocks]. Subtract.

Show.	Do you need to regroup?	Subtract the ones. Write how many tens and ones are left.
9 28 − 9 = ____	Yes No	____ tens ____ ones
10 32 − 17 = ____	Yes No	____ tens ____ ones

Subtract.

11
```
  74
−  2
────
```

12
```
  74
− 20
────
```

13

tens	ones
□	□
5	2
−3	6

14

tens	ones
□	□
4	0
−	3

15 Rewrite.
Then subtract.

34 − 28

tens	ones
□	□
−	

16 Subtract. Add to check.

```
  22
− 14
────
```

Problem Solving

17 Jennifer wants to buy crayons for 45¢. She has 32¢. How much more money does she need?

____ ¢

Name ______________________________

Performance Assessment
Unit 3

Book Fair

Zack and his brother Jacob went to the book fair at the library.

- Zack had 52¢ and Jacob had 38¢.
- They put their money together and bought 2 items.
- They spent a total of 71¢.

Which 2 items could they have bought? How much change did they have left?

Show your work.

Technology

Name ______________________

Calculator • Make the Next Number

Use a .
Add or subtract to get to each number.

23 ◯ ____ = 53 ◯ ____ = 31

Step 1

Think: 23 < 53, so add.

Press ON/C 2 3 + 3 0 = | 53 |.

Step 2

Think: 53 > 31, so subtract.

Press − 2 2 = | 31 |.

So, 23 + 30 = 53 − 22 = 31

Practice and Problem Solving

Use a .
Add or subtract to get to each number.

1. 65 ◯ ____ = 35 ◯ ____ = 38 ◯ ____ = 78

Make your own.

2. ____ ◯ ____ = ____ ◯ ____ = ____

3. **Talk About It** Explain how to get from 23 to 73 to 78 to 68.

Name ______________________________

PROBLEM SOLVING ON LOCATION

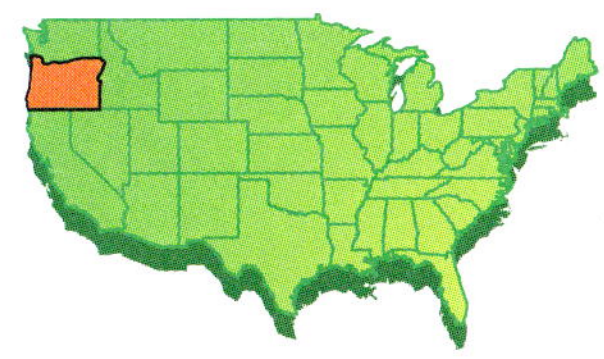

On the Trail

Pioneer families traveled by wagon and by foot on the Oregon trail. They carried with them all they owned.

Each wagon holds 100 pounds. Find a way to load every item onto the wagons. Draw and label different ways.

Name ________________________________

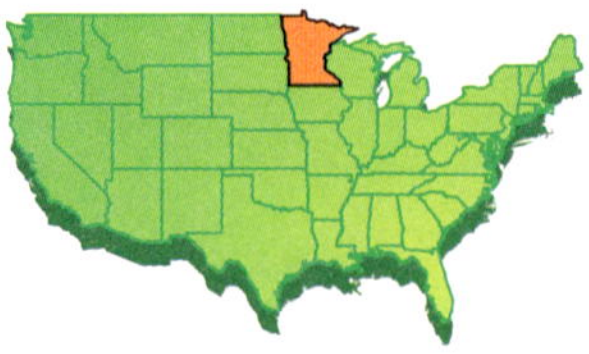

PROBLEM SOLVING ON LOCATION

On the Road

Chippewa National Forest, in Minnesota, is a favorite place for hiking, camping, swimming, boating, and fishing.

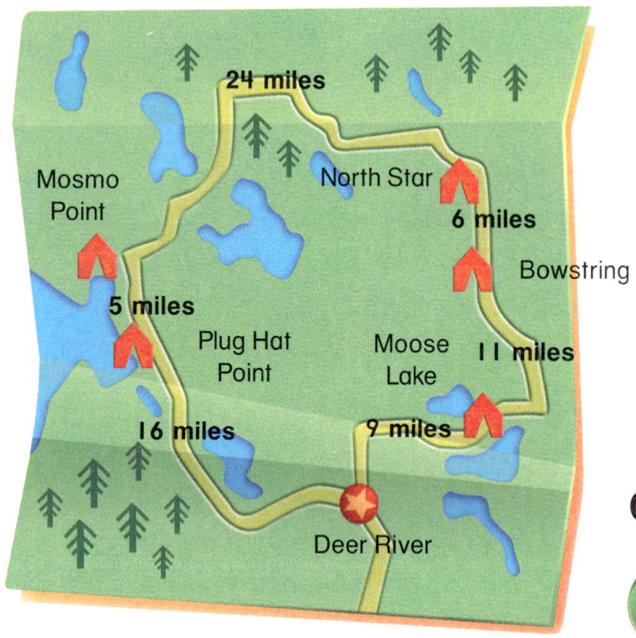

Chippewa National Forest

= campsite

Plan a 5-day camping trip. Start at Deer River, and end at Deer River. Go on to a new campsite each day. Complete the chart.

	From	To	Miles
Day 1	Deer River		
Day 2			
Day 3			
Day 4			
Day 5			
Day 6		Deer River	
		Total miles traveled	